DO-IT-YOURSELF BLACK BEAR BAITING AND HUNTING

by

Dr. Ken Nordberg

Artwork by Buzz Buczynski
Photos by Jene Kathryn Armstrong & Dr. Ken Nordberg
Edited by M. C. O'Donnell

Published by
SHINGLE CREEK OUTDOOR PRODUCTIONS
Minneapolis

Copyright © 1990 by Shingle Creek Outdoor Productions
LIBRARY OF CONGRESS CATALOGUE CARD NUMBER
ISBN00000000

Manufactured in the United States of America

Dedication

To the rainbow of my life,

Jene Kathryn

—pathfinder, adventurer and gentle tamer of wild beasts

Acknowledgements

A "special" thanks to:

Lynn L. Rogers, noted black bear biologist of the U.S. Forest Service, North Central Forest Experiment Station, 1992 Folwell Avenue, St. Paul, Minnesota 55108, for information concerning the natural history of the black bear.

Wisconsin Department of Natural Resources, Bureau of Wildlife Managment for statistics and other information concerning the lives of black bears.

Richard P. Smith, author of *The Book of the Black Bear* a source of boundless information about black bears.

Wade Nolan, friend, noted wildlife video photographer and bear hunter from Girdwood, Alaska for information presented in his most excellent video, "Bowhunting Hungry Black Bears."

Buzz Buczynski, friend and artist extraordinaire for creating artwork vital to this book.

My sons, John, Dave and Ken, and my son-in-law, Kevin Stone, for the many vital roles they played in making this book possible.

Jene Kathryn Armstrong for her wonderful wildlife photography and unflagging aid and dedication throughout the creation of this book.

CONTENTS

Foreword xiii
Introduction 1
   Ken's First Bear 1

Chapter 1: Things Hunters Should Know About Black Bears ... 7
   Sizes and Weights 7
   Sex Characteristics 9
   Longevity 9
   Coloration 9
   Speed 9
   Paws 9
   Breeding 10
   Gestation 10
   Cubs, Yearlings and Subadults 10
   Denning 11
   Home Ranges 11
   Feeding Cycles 13
   Some Factors That Influence the Timing of Feeding Cycles 14
      Winds 14
      Precipitation 14
      Human Activities 15
   Are Black Bears Dangerous? 15
      The Bear on the Knoll 18
      The Bear That Came to Breakfast 19
   Antidote for Danger 21

Chapter 2: Locating Productive Bait/Stand Sites 23
   "Scattergun" Approach 23
   "Let the Bears Do the Walking" Approach 23
   "Go to the Bears" Approach 24
   Where to Look for Bear Signs 25
   Where Dogs Are Used to Hunt Black Bears 29
   Recognizing and Interpreting Bear Signs 30
      Bear Tracks 31
      Bear Droppings 32
      Signs of Feeding 34
      Bear (Scratch) Trees 36
      Dens 38
   Mapping Bear Signs 38
   Prerequisites of Productive Bait/Stand Sites 38
      Adequate Bear Cover 38
      Adequate Stand Cover 39
      Minimal Change 39
      Undisturbed Bears 40
      Quick Transport of Carcass 41

Multiple Bait/Stand Sites and Distances Between Stands 41

Chapter 3: Bait/Stand Site Preparation 43
    Black-Bear-Effective Stands 43
    Dave's Trembling Balsam 43
    Essential Bait/Stand Site Elements 44
    When to Prepare a Bait/Stand Site 44
        Stand Site Preparation 45
        Stand Positioning 45
        Stand Height 46
        Stand Camouflage 47
        Stand Comfort and Silence 48
        Stand Safety 48
    Bait Site Preparation 48
    Dave's First Bear 51
    Shooting Lane Preparation 53
    Stand Trail Preparation 54
    Bait Storage 55

Chapter 4: Baits and Baiting Tactics 57
    Elements of Effectiveness 58
        Competitive 58
        Holding Power 58
        Latent Attraction 59
        Mask Human Odors 59
        Long-Range Attraction 59
    Recommended Baits 59
        Meats 59
        Vegetables and Grain 60
        Fruits 61
        Sweets 61
        Cooking Oils and Greases 62
    Baiting Tactics 63
        How to Provide Baits 63
        Time of Day to Provide Baits 65
        The Rule of Six 65
        Bait Amounts and Frequency of Baiting 65

Chapter 5: Preparing to Hunt Black Bears 69
    Effective Weaponry 69
        Points to Consider 69
        Exit Wound Capability 70
        The Myth of Firepower 70
        Risky Head and Neck Shots 71
        String Trackers 71
        Recommended Weaponry 72

Developing "Perfect Bear Shot" Marksmanship 73
   Develop a Shooting Groove 74
   Become an Expert Marksman 75
   Recognize Effective Heart Shot Angles 78
   Concentrate on Making the Shot 78
Hunting Gear 80
Personal Scent Management 86
Bear Camp 86
   John's Surprise 87
Pre-Hunt Planning 89
   Length of Hunt 89
   Hunting Hours 90
   Meals 91
   Baiting Hours 91
   Bear Carcass Preservation 91
   Ready at Last 92

Chapter 6: Hunting Blacks Bears over Bait 93
From Camper/Baiter to Black Bear Hunter 93
   Body and Clothing 93
   Boots 93
   Headwear 94
   Standpack Gear 94
   Applying Camo to Exposed Skin 94
   Cover Scent 95
   Preparing Your Weapon 96
From Camp to Stand 98
   The Direct Approach 98
   The Noisy, Two-Man Approach 98
   The Silent Approach 98
   The Beginning Trail 99
   The Middle Trail 99
   The End Trail 100
   Sounds That Identify Humans 101
   A Bear at the Pit 102
From Stand Trail to Stand Platform 104
   Using a Bear Lure 104
   Honey Burn 105
   Preparing a Weapon for Hauling up to a Stand 106
   Climbing to Stand Platform 106
   Buckling Up 107
   Hauling Up a Weapon 107
Preparing for a Long Vigil 107
Preparing a Firearm for the Shot 108
Preparing Archery Gear for the Shot 109
Preparing Other Gear 109

ix

Rain 109
Cooling Temperatures 110
Direct Sunlight 110
Biting Insects 111
Detecting Approaching Black Bears 111
How Black Bears Approach Bait Pits 113
    Kevin's Lost Arrow 113
Avoiding a Black Bear's Sixth Sense 114
The Shot 115
Responses of Black Bears to Hits 118
    Heart/Lung Hits 118
    Other Hits 118
After the Shot 119
    When to Begin Tracking 120
    Recovering a Shot Black Bear 121
    Three Rules for Safe and Effective Tracking 121
    Trail Signs of Wounded Bears 122
        Blood 122
        Hair 123
        Bone 124
        Other Bodily Substances 124
        Other Trail Signs 124
    200-Plus-Yard Trails 125
    Lost Trail 125
    When All Else Fails 126
    Night Tracking 126
Approaching a Downed Black Bear 127
Finishing Shots — Downed Bears 127
Finishing Shots — Moving Bears 128
The Almost Mythical Charge 128
Kill Site Photos 129

Chapter 7: Black Bear Harvest 131
Field Dressing 131
Transporting Your Bear to Camp 142
    A Bear Too Big to Handle 142
    Dragging 142
Field and Camo Care of a Bear Carcass 143
Emergency Measures for Saving Bear Hide and Meat 144
Transporting Your Bear in a Vehicle 145
Skinning 145
    Bear Rug Skinning 146
    Shoulder Mount Skinning 148
    Full Mount Skinning 149
Mounts with Snarling Lips 149
Butchering 150

    Loins 151
    Round Steaks 151
    Shoulders 151
    Everything Else 151
    Trophy Bear Measurements 152
    Bear Meat Magic 152
        Eyebrow-Raising Bear Steaks 153
        Mother Nature's Finest Stew 153
        Black Bear Roast 155
        Ground Bear 156

Epilogue: It Doesn't Get Any Better 157

Bibliography 161

FOREWORD

This book can make a dramatic difference in how much you enjoy hunting black bear. It's packed with information gained first-hand about the habits of adult bruins, some of the smartest, shyest and most awe-inspiring game animals you'll ever pursue.

While the author has been known more for his books, seminars and Bowhunting World columns on whitetails, the forest "laboratory" he studies in for several months each year is also home to a healthy black bear population. It was natural for Dr. Ken Nordberg to get bit by the bear-hunting bug and then to question conventional wisdom about how to find and fool ever-larger specimens.

Last fall, at a distance of five yards, Dr. Nordberg arrowed his largest black bear ever. The 422-pound bruin was patterned as surely as any trophy buck, and fell to a combination of skill in scouting, baiting and shot placement that this book can help you to obtain.

Tim Dehn, Managing Editor
Bowhunting World Magazine
Wayzata, Minnesota

INTRODUCTION

This is a book of extraordinary hunting adventure — hair-raising, heart-thumping, knee-knocking, explosively exciting adventure — *black bear hunting adventure*. Celebrated American hunters Daniel Boone and Davy Crockett considered facing a big black bear, one-on-one, to be a true test of a hunter's mettle. No doubt about it, it's an enormous personal challenge all right, crackling with suspense, electrifying excitement and an unavoidable feeling of danger.

Having often experienced the full range of emotions that are ever a part of black bear hunting myself, I knew writing a book of black bear hunting instruction would not be easy. I knew I'd have to accomplish much more than simply explain hunting-related black bear behavior patterns, big-bear-effective scouting methods, baits, baiting tactics and hunting techniques. To have bone fide value (for both hunters and black bears), I'd have to put hunters face-to-face with black bears. I'd have to make sure they know exactly how it feels. Only then could hunters fully understand why they must develop exceptional skills for hunting black bears — *why they must become the very best.*

In this spirit, this step-by-step guide to hunting black bears with firearm or bow is written for beginners, experienced do-it-yourselfers and professional guides. It will teach first-timers how to key on braggin'-sized black bears from the outset. For experienced do-it-yourselfers, it will open the door to large-to-very-large bruins. It will provide professionals with more effective means of guiding clients to trophy-class bears. For all, it will lead to safe, no-waste harvests of one the world's most revered big game animals.

If you are a first-timer, anticipating your very first hunt for black bears, I guarantee you're in for a surprise. Black bear hunting is like no other hunting. You're going to call your very first hunt "an adventure of a lifetime," likely much more than you bargained on. Take my son Ken's first black bear hunt:

Ken's First Bear

It was 5PM. Ken and I were fast slipping toward the "downright miserable" mark on the human comfort scale. During the previous 2-1/2 hours, our rain gear had proven to be adequate for only about half of a thunderous, 3-inch rainfall. Unaffected by the rain, industrious hordes of savage mosquitoes hungrily invaded every lap of our clothing and netting. One dubious grace up until this moment was provided by the maple stand railings upon which we sat. Broad and comfortable at first, they had become so knife-edged and knobby that we hardly noticed we were shivering and bleeding from dozens of welts.

Then things changed. We suddenly felt more determined than ever to maintain our quiet, motionless vigil within the somewhat cramped confines of our ancient tree stand — me with my plastic-wrapped camera gear in hand and Ken with his rifle. The reason for this renewed resolve (or lunacy) was threefold: 1) the rain had subsided to a mere steady drizzle, 2) two foraging Canada jays had just landed at our bait pit (meaning forest creatures were beginning their end-of-the-day quest for food) and 3) we both had this growing feeling inside: *something is about to happen!* Where such a feeling comes from, I'm not sure. It may be purely a matter of intuition, or perhaps it's an experienced hunter's mind subconsciously recognizing the elements that add up to "this is the right time and this is the right place." At any rate, as fitful zephyrs dislodged cascades of enormous, back-splattering raindrops from the frost-touched canopy of birches overhead, the air about us began to fairly crackle with anticipation. So much so that we were no longer conscious of our physical discomforts.

Though my youngest son was by now a well-seasoned whitetail hunter, I knew from experience his unspoken feelings at this time. "Awestricken" comes close to being the right term for it. The moment was near at hand when he would face one of the world's largest land carnivores — a powerful and swift creature endowed with fearsome claws and fangs; one that could easily climb to our perch and wreck havoc, if so inclined; one that not uncommonly instills astonishing fear among the most stalwart of outdoorspersons. Having never faced a bear with the intention of shooting it before, an inexperienced bear hunter will certainly be plagued by disquieting thoughts.

"Will I remain calm and collected?" one can't help but wonder. *"What will happen if I goof, merely wounding one, or what will happen if a sow with cubs shows up?"*

You keep reminding yourself (as others keep insisting) black bears are harmless, but without bear hunting experience, such assurances can never fully dispel that very-human, deeply-ingrained fear of bears. Anticipating that first bear, then, is not unlike anticipating a first battle. Knowing it will be soon, the first-timer cannot help but sweat a bit and worry, keeping some fingers mentally crossed.

For several minutes Ken and I watched the antics of the two hungry jays hopping excitedly about the tightly spaced logs lying over our bait pit. Down through the cracks between the logs they could see a veritable treasure of enticing foods — meat scraps, suet, apples, blueberry preserves, pastries and such.

Suddenly the jays flushed, scolding raucously.

"Something's coming," I whispered.

"Over on the right," Ken shortly hissed.

Within a dense patch of sodden hazels some fifty yards away, I caught a glimpse of a dark form ghosting silently nearer, its path revealed by parting hazels. Moments later, a large, tawny-muzzled, black head emerged from the thick hazels at the edge of the small opening surrounding our bait pit. Smallish, brown eyes beneath tawny brow dots intently swept the area, lingering a bit on the two breathless, camo-clad forms seated on a platform six feet up in an adjacent cluster of birches. At length satisfied, a black bear stepped into the clearing, pausing to vigorously shake rainwater from its fur. Then a second bruin unexpectedly burst from the hazels.

Ken slowly turned his head, eyes wide, questioning.

"Yearlings," I mouthed, shaking my head slightly from side-to-side. Much larger bears were visiting this bait site. Ken could afford to be fussy.

The twin bears, Black-Lab-sized (about 100 pounds each), pounced eagerly on the 100-pound-plus logs covering our pit. They effortlessly rolled three of them to one side, exposing the cache of food. Crowding into the opening, they noisily lapped blueberry preserves for a few minutes and then snatched up meaty beef bones, rushing with their prizes to opposite sides of the clearing.

Every few minutes, one bear or the other quit its hungry gnawing and rose upright on hind paws to study its surroundings. The probable reason for this nervous behavior became evident some twenty minutes later.

"Urr-OOF!" something previously unnoticed uttered from almost directly beneath our stand. Hair standing on end (a universal affliction among all small bears and humans present), the yearlings immediately dropped their bones and sprinted south, appearing from behind like two bouncing, black rubber beach balls.

Seconds later, a glaring, scar-faced, chocolate-colored brute charged malevolently into the clearing. Normally, the mere appearance of a mature black bear is enough to start one's heart thumping, and knees trembling, but this one — some 250-pounds of fulminating inferno — cast an added complexion on matters. Even though black bears, as a rule, are extremely unlikely to vent anger on humans, at this particular moment a couple of Nordberg's — mouths agape — could not escape the feeling there might be some exceptions to this rule.

"There's your bear," I needn't have choked — Ken's Browning was already half-way to his shoulder. As he frantically wiped fog and drizzle from the lenses of his scope, the bruin moved to the nearby bear scratch tree upon which we had earlier poured honey. Noting the bear was now partially screened by intervening branches and foliage, I nudged Ken with a knee. Ken understood, nodding. With *any* bear this would've been a risky shot, one best avoided. With this bear...well, it (the shot) had to be *perfect*.

Five, suspense-racked minutes passed before the bear finally licked the scratch tree clean. Then — heavy thunder again rumbling in the west — the bear stalked to the pit. Before reaching for a pirated morsel, however, it paused, standing head-up, broadside, glaring in the direction taken by the terrified yearlings.

The hush of the dripping forest was shattered by the deafening blast of Ken's 7mm Magnum. Commencing immediately thereafter: 1) the heart-shot, chocolate-brown bear barreled into the thick hazels on our right, 2) one of the yearlings reappeared, streaking directly toward our stand, 3) a bolt of lightening stabbed through the crown of a nearby pine, showering the forest floor with sparks not far behind the oncoming yearling, 4) upon lurching to our feet (Ken ejecting his spent cartridge), that portion of the years-old stand platform beneath my feet cracked, 5) the unseen chocolate-brown bear began to roar, and 6) I abruptly found myself dangling from my armpits, startled by the realization that my legs were suddenly within an easy chomp of at least two crazed bears — one unseen but obviously very near (judging by its horrendous roars) and the other closing very rapidly.

Happily, the confused yearling spooked at the sight of my flailing legs (whereupon it tore open a new path in yet another direction) and the chocolate-brown bruin succumbed during its third roar.

This exciting episode was the Nordberg family's introduction to do-it-yourself bear hunting, launching my sons, son-in-law and I into a very successful decade of bear hunting adventure. Previous to this hunt

Ken's chocolate-brown bruin dropped 35 yards from bait pit.

— made possible by Ken's successful drawing of a permit to take part in Minnesota's first, quota-type bear hunt — I had occasionally booked guided bear hunts in Canada, not always with success. Borrowing the best of what I had learned from professional bear guides and then adding some tricks of my own (based on long-term observations of abundant black bears within my north-central Minnesota whitetail study area), we were at once successful; so successful that during the 30 hours preceding the taking of the chocolate-brown bruin we had attracted eleven different bears to Ken's two bait/stand sites. Except at northern Minnesota landfills, I had never seen (and photographed) so many black bears in so short a period of time.

Since that first do-it-yourself hunt, we have drawn 1-4 permits annually (except once) and we've either been 100% successful within 36 hours of the September 1st opener, or we easily could have been. In recent years — bowhunting only — we have declined many opportunities to take small-to-medium-sized bears (up to 300 pounds). Today, we concentrate on more-challenging, larger bears, and we've been successful at that. With our success, we've proved beyond a doubt that do-it-yourselfers can easily enjoy hunting adventures as great as there are to be found in the world today.

Teaching others what I knew about black bears and black bear hunting had long been on my mind. In fact, most of the bear hunting research my sons, son-in-law and I conducted over the past decade was intended to provide effective tips and instructions for a book. I have always felt a certain reluctance to write such a book, however. I knew what I could share would substantially increase man-bear confrontations. I also harbored some fears about what the consequences might be. I really like black bears. I like to be among them I like to see them in our wilds, I thoroughly enjoy hunting them and I prefer wilderness black bear loin steaks over all others. I hate the thought of contributing in any way to anything that might in the least threaten the future of black bears. I knew, therefore, that along with teaching others how to more successfully hunt black bears, I'd somehow have to teach them how to hunt black bears responsibly. This may seem simple and logical enough, but regardless of what anyone says, when hunters meet bears, good sense and responsible thoughts tend to fade very quickly. Black bear hunting being a highly emotional experience — typically stupefying and physically debilitating — I knew I'd also have to teach hunters how to control their emotions when facing a bear. I'm still not sure that's entirely possible.

What finally prompted me to begin writing this book was the mind-boggling number of "crippling-loss" and "spoiled-carcass" horror stories I heard last fall. Suddenly, it became manifestly evident average bear hunters today are in almost desperate need of good and sensible hunting instructions. This need is reflected by three facts: 1) the vast majority of black bears taken by hunters today are young and small (less than five years of age and less than 200 pounds), 2) too many black bears are being wasted and 3) too many hunters are treating black bears foolishly, inviting unnecessary danger. With do-it-yourself black bear hunting growing in popularity as it is, these wrongs must be corrected or black bears and black bear hunting will soon be facing an uncertain future, and increasing numbers of hunters are going to be injured by black bears.

Most tragic is "waste." The number-one cause of waste is inept field marksmanship. Unfortunately, inept, emotionally-impaired marksmanship is almost a "gimme" in black bear hunting.

The trouble is, black bears are nowhere as abundant and never as prolific as other popular big game animals. It is estimated there are only about 500,000 black bears in forty U.S. states (including Alaska) and all

Canadian provinces today (Nolan and Ertz 1987). Though this most common species of North American bears is holding its own — even increasing in numbers in some areas — overall, that's not a lot of bears. Unlikely to ever become significantly more abundant than they are today, these wonderful trophy animals are in danger of being over-exploited in a way that cannot be easily measured (crippling-losses), if at all. Given valuable opportunities to harvest black bears within biologically-sound limits, we hunters must be preservation-minded. Especially with black bears, we cannot countenance wasteful hunting. *We cannot afford to wound and lose a single black bear. We must make every shot count.*

Given these facts, most hunters would heartily agree black bears should not be wasted, but as most who are experienced in bear hunting know, making a perfect shot can be an awesome challenge. Though it can be done — routinely — the casual approach to marksmanship so typical of whitetail hunters today is wholly inadequate for bear hunting. We black bear hunters must be very serious about what we are doing. We must be knowledgeable, very good shots, well-prepared and well-equipped. It's not only a matter of avoiding danger — it's a matter of assuring the future of black bears and black bear hunting.

There was one other reason I have long felt somewhat reluctant to write this book — I knew I'd be obliged to take up an unpopular opinion toward black bears. Based on personal experiences, I could not in good conscience agree with those who insist "black bears are completely harmless." Typically, in consequence of misconceptions, a lack of hunting savvy and/or disrespectful attitudes toward black bears, hunters blunder. Some blunders can lead hunters into some rather harrowing situations with black bears. As a longtime observer (non-threatening) of black bears, I know I can approach black bears without danger. As a longtime hunter of black bears, however, I also know hunters who somehow threaten or challenge black bears can sometimes elicit hostile responses. Moreover, inexperienced hunters are not apt to recognize when it is prudent to back off, or how. No matter how slight the potential, I believe foolish or uninformed hunters can be injured by black bears, especially by wounded, dominant black bears. When hunted properly, and when the hunter has the right attitude toward these swift and powerful beasts, I believe the likelihood of being injured by a black bear is no greater than the likelihood of being injured by a white-tailed buck.

I want no one I teach to be injured by a black bear. Thus, though many may insist black bears are completely harmless, and though some may even seek to discredit my stand on this point, I for one can only teach others to hunt black bears as I personally hunt black bears — treat them as if they are *indeed dangerous*. Therein, I believe, lies safety in black bear hunting. As for those who chose to hunt black bears as if they are completely harmless, or, as for those who choose to teach others to hunt black bears as if they are completely harmless, all I can say is, "Beware."

Chapter 1

Things Hunters Should Know About Black Bears

Sizes and Weights

Weights of black bears are easy to figure. Most seen in the woods weigh 500-600 pounds. For some strange reason, however, most black bears shot by hunters weigh 225-300 pounds, except, of course, the ones that get away. They generally weigh 500-600 pounds. Oddly, almost all scales used to weigh black bears are defective (probably caked inside with rust). Black bears obviously weighing 225-300 pounds could not possibly weigh only 100-170 pounds. Who ever heard of a hunter seeing black bears weighing less than 500-600 pounds, or of a hunter shooting a black bear weighing less than 225-300 pounds?

Are most claimed weights of black bears *fish stories*? Probably. The problem is, black bears characteristically appear to be much larger than they really are. Though the average adult black bear may only measure 60 inches from nose-to-tail and 25 inches at the shoulder, such a bear will have a neck that appears to be much larger in diameter than its head, a rump that appears to be as wide as the rump of a Black Angus, and legs that appear to be as big around as powder kegs. A human with such characteristics is likely to weigh well over 200 pounds; maybe close to 300 pounds. Many Minnesota white-tailed bucks weigh 305 pounds (dressing out at about 245 pounds). Though a black bear does not have as long a neck, nor as as long legs, the body of a 250-pound bear will appear to be much heavier than the body of a 305-pound buck. It'll feel heavier too, being much more difficult to drag. Add to a bear a smooth and deep pelt and a belly that hangs almost to the ground and you've got a 250-pound animal that easily appears to weigh 400 pounds; maybe even 500 pounds. This optical illusion makes bear registration station scales the most unbelievable scales in the world.

When more than one bear is present, it is easy to make comparisons — a big one will appear "big." Except for sows with cubs, however, rarely will a hunter see more than one black bear at a bait site at one time. Unless the bear is a cub, it can appear "big" whatever it's actual size. Even a yearling can appear "big" if it's fat and has a thick pelt. This easy mistake, plus the fact that younger black bears are by far the most common visitors at bait sites during legal shooting hours, largely accounts for the fact that most black bears taken by hunters actually do weigh only 100-170 pounds dressed. Some even weigh substantially less than 100 pounds. Of course, black bears do lose weight when field dressed, but only about 15% for small-to-medium-sized bears and about 10% for large-to-very-large bears. Finding the *actual* weight hard to believe, hating to admit they were fooled and hearing everyone else talk about taking 225-300 pound bears, few hunters are inclined to back off from their original estimates of the sizes of the bears they have taken. If black bears had antlers, providing a quick and easy index of size, likely more hunters would take bears that actually do weigh 225-300 pounds, this weight range being fairly common among black bears.

Average adult males — 4 years of age or older — measure 54-70 inches nose-to-tail and weigh 250-350 pounds. Some boars attain weights of 400-600 pounds or more. The heaviest on record weighed 802-1/2 pounds live (shot near Stevens Point, Wisconsin in 1885). Average adult females measure 50-58 inches in length and weigh 120-180 pounds (Wise 1986). Adult males generally weigh 50-100% more than adult females. Yearlings measure about four feet in length and weigh about 100-125 pounds (fall), males being heavier. Anything smaller is a cub.

Alongside six-foot logs, these bears prove to be yearlings.

Without some sort of an aid, it is always difficult, if not impossible, to accurately estimate the size of an individual black bear. In the excitement of a near encounter, physical appearances are not particularly reliable. Ears that appear small is a widely accepted characteristic of larger bears (smaller bears having ears that appear large), but a thick pelt on a small bear can be a fooler. Some years (when food is scarce) bears can appear lanky and their ears will appear large; other years they can be especially fat and their ears will appear small. For that matter, it is not uncommon to see wide differences in weight (fatness) and in the thickness of fur among bears in the same area.

Having been fooled often enough myself, some years ago I began searching for a more reliable method of sizing up solitary bears at bait sites. One day, while cutting logs to lay over a bait pit, I was suddenly struck with a simple answer — cut six-foot-long logs. I have never since failed to accurately estimate the relative size of a black bear. It works like this: when standing parallel to one of these logs, the largest sow or

250-pound boar will be about one foot shorter, nose to tail. A 300-350 pounder will be about 3-6 inches shorter. A 400-450 pound bear will about equal the length of these logs. A bear that is significantly longer, is truly a "big" black bear. Any bruin that equals or is is longer than a six-foot log is a potential "record book" bear. That's about all a hunter really needs to know about bear sizes.

Sex Characteristics

From an elevated stand, it can be nearly impossible to determine whether a black bear is a male or female — essentially, their bodies are identical. On some males, the penis is obvious. On nursing females, breasts — located on the chest (like humans) — will appear enlarged and scantily furred. If you have a bear before you that is not accompanied by cubs and it is more than five feet long from nose to tail (according to your pit logs), you can bet it's a boar.

Longevity

Though few black bears survive beyond age 20, some live 30-40 years in the wilds (Rogers 1987; Smith 1985). Extreme age is not necessarily a prerequisite to being a record book bear. Boars 6-1/2 years of age can have skulls that qualify for the Pope and Young record book (18+ inches).

Coloration

Though there are at least 18 recognized subspecies of black bears, the most common and widespread is *Ursus americanus*. In the eastern half of North America, 99% of black bears are black with tawny muzzles. West of the Mississippi, brown phases — cinnamon, chocolate and blond — are more common (Smith 1985).

Speed

Black bears can attain speeds of 30 mph or more (Wise 1986).

Paws

Black bears walk on leathery soles that resemble the soles of humans. Each paw has five toes and each toe is equipped with a curved, non-retractable claw. Sharp and tough, a black bear's claws are used to dispatch live prey, to tear apart rotten logs (searching for insects), to excavate dens, ant hills, roots and rodent burrows and to climb trees.

Breeding

Black bears breed from May through August, peak months being May and June. Most females do not breed for the first time until they are 3-4 years of age; most males, not until age 4-5. Mature sows normally produce young every other year, not experiencing estrus while nursing young during intervening years. When natural food production is inadequate, some sows may skip a year or two. When in estrus, males are attracted to widely traveling females via trail scent. In estrus only 2-3 days, a female will breed several times, sometimes with more than one male. Battles are most common among boars of the same size when attracted to the same sow (Rogers.1987; Smith 1985).

Gestation

Once successfully bred, in vitro cub development (taking 225 days) occurs in two stages. First, fertilized eggs develop into a blastocysts which are stored in a liquid within the uterus. Further development does not occur until a sow is in its winter den. During late November or early December, blastocysts become implanted in the uterine wall and final development begins. One to five blind and nearly hairless, 6-8 inch-long cubs weighing a mere 7-12 ounces are born 6-8 weeks later, usually during January or February. In the eastern half of the black bear's geographic range, litters of 2-3 cubs are most common; 1-2 in the western half. By the time cubs emerge from their dens in the spring, they weigh 5-10 pounds, depending on the size of the litter (Rogers 1987; Wise 1986).

Cubs, Yearlings and Subadults

Cubs generally nurse until August and sometimes into September, closely following their mothers throughout their first year. Most begin eating some solid foods during mid-summer. Cubs den with their mothers during their second winter. After emerging from dens in the spring, shortly before breeding begins the young bears — now referred to as "yearlings" — are driven off or abandoned by their mothers. Yearlings generally disperse a short distance, establishing small (247-1730 acre), exclusive (avoided by their mothers) home ranges within portions of their mothers' home ranges. When subadult (non-breeding) two-year-olds, most males (some wait until age 3 or 4) disperse an average of 33 miles and establish new, permanent home ranges. Females generally remain in the area in which they were born, establishing exclusive home ranges that usually include portions of home ranges ceded voluntarily by their mothers (Rogers 1987).

Denning

Except in the deep south, black bears hibernate (sleep deeply) during the winter months. While hibernating in more northern latitudes, their heart and breathing rates slow and body temperatures drop, greatly reducing their caloric needs. Not consuming foods during the period of hibernation, nourishment comes from fat stores accumulated during late summer and fall. By the time black bears emerge from their dens in the spring, nursing sows have lost 30-35% of their total pre-denning weight; males about 20%.

Black bears den in small caves dug into the sides of slopes, under brush piles, windfalls, tree roots or old buildings, in hollow trees (sometimes off the ground) and occasionally even in culverts. Some merely curl up in a nest on the ground where they are eventually covered by snow.

Where winters are longer, such as in Alaska, black bears begin hibernation as early as October, not emerging from dens until late April or early May. Across the northern half of the U.S., most bears enter their dens from late September to mid-November, emerging in late March or April. In more southern states, denning may not begin until late December, bears emerging in March. Denning may begin earlier than normal when natural foods are scarce in the fall. (Smith 1985)

Home Ranges

A knowledge of home range distribution, sizes and utilization is important to success when hunting trophy-class black bears (older boars).

Having observed many bears within my whitetails study area over a period of 21 years, I long ago came to realize black bears establish individual home ranges like white-tailed deer — areas in which individual bears forage and den throughout their lives, as long as food, water and cover remain adequate. Though I have tried on several occasions, however, I have never succeeded in measuring a black bear home range. Based on admittedly "fragmentary" observations of identifiable (having unique white patches on breasts) bears at various sites over considerable periods of time, I came to realize older boars have enormous home ranges — two had ranges at least 8-10 miles long east and west with undetermined widths north and south. Some older boars visited bait sites up to eight miles apart. One was identified at sites ten miles apart. Like the home ranges of white-tailed bucks, individual boar home ranges seemed to overlap considerably with the ranges of other male bears, each doubtless encompassing a fair number of smaller female home ranges. This accounts for sightings of up to 2-4 male bears at some bait sites within 2-4 days of initial baiting.

As near as I could figure, mature sows maintained home ranges that were much smaller — about 2-3 miles long in one direction and 2 miles wide, making them about 4-6 square-miles in size. Like adult white-tailed does, adult sows seemed to establish home ranges exclusive of other adult sows, accounting for the fact that we never saw more than one sow with cubs at any one bait site. Some bait sites slightly more than two miles apart were regularly visited by the same sow with cubs. Bait sites three or more miles apart were never visited by the same sow with cubs.

Another curious thing we noted was, that while we commonly sighted younger emancipated bears (male and female yearlings and bears a year or two older) during separate intervals at bait pits regularly visited by sows with cubs — these sites drawing multiple bears like a dump — these sites were never visited by larger boars. It seemed sows with young were able to keep larger boars — perhaps predators of cubs — out of their home ranges.

At the same time, we never saw any other bears of any kind, including sows with cubs, at bait sites regularly visited by very large (probably dominant) boars. Having seen other bears near such sites at other times of the year, but never sows, two things seemed apparent: 1) larger, dominant boars are able to intimidate younger bears — via scent (urine) or running them off — effectively enough to keep them away, even over 3-4 day periods while larger boars are foraging elsewhere, and 2) such sites were not within the bounds of sow home ranges.

Based on the above observations, I came to the following conclusions: *1) baits sites located within 4-6 square-mile areas known to be inhabited by sows with cubs are likely to draw several black bears, but none large, and 2) bait sites intended to draw larger boars should be located outside of 4-6 square-mile areas known to be inhabited by sows with cubs.*

To successfully hunt trophy-class black bears, then, the hunter must scout for bear signs — distinguishing large-bear from sow-with-cub signs — before deciding on where to prepare bait/stand sites.

As we further learned, boar bait/stand sites are likely to be effective for taking boars year after year, black bear home ranges apparently being situated in the same geographic regions year after year and each apparently being adopted by other bears (of the same sex) when they become empty for one reason or another (usually due to hunting).

According to a long-term (1969-1985) northeastern Minnesota black bear study by Lynn L. Rogers of the U.S. Forest Service, females that have borne cubs have home ranges that average 3.7 square-miles in size; non-breeding females average 2.8 square-miles. Except near large dumps, adjacent sow home ranges did not overlap, sows vigorously defended the bounds of their ranges against invasions by other female bears. Adult boars had overlapping ranges that averaged 29 square-miles in size. Except when sows were in estrus, adult boars did not intrude on sow ranges. (Rogers 1987)

Feeding Cycles

The cycles during which black bears are active — primarily feeding (during hunting seasons) — are not as predictable in onset and duration as the feeding cycles of white-tailed deer. This is largely due to the fact that black bear foods are not as reliably available nor as abundant as whitetail foods during spring or fall. When foods are particularly scarce, black bears may be on the move during any hour of the day or night. Even then, however, peak feeding hours tend to occur early and late in the day — during periods of subdued light.

A relative abundance of foods, or a relative scarcity, can also dramatically change the distribution and numbers of bears in any one area. For example, if foods become scarce where black bears are normally abundant, within a very short time the area can become virtually devoid of bears. Black bears are known to migrate great distances (sometimes more than 100 miles) in quest of food, returning in the fall to their usual ranges for denning. Bait pits are unlikely to hold black bears long in an area where natural foods are inadequate.

Sometimes special foods will draw bears from normal ranges, holding and concentrating them temporarily where bears are not normally common. In September of 1987, for example, hunters over much of Minnesota were puzzled by the absence of bears during the first two weeks of the hunting season, especially after having plenty of bears regularly hit bait pits during the previous two weeks. What happened? A heavy crop of wild cranberries (at least in Aitkin County) had attracted black bears in mass to bogs, and the bears stayed there until the cranberries were no longer available.

When wild foods are relatively abundant, black bear feeding cycles are fairly predictable, perhaps "normal." Then, they are like whitetail feeding cycles, a morning cycle beginning about two hours before sunrise and lasting until about two hours after sunrise; an afternoon cycle beginning about 2-3 hours before sunset and continuing until about two hours after sunset. Younger adult bears (not including cubs tend to spend more time field during daylight hours than older bears. As black bears age, they seem to spend less and less time moving about by day. Many older boars become almost completely nocturnal, except when food is scarce. Nocturnal bears may be spotted moving (or visiting camp) up to four hours before sunrise and up to four hours after sunset. Whatever the conditions, if there is one daylight hour during which older black bears can most be counted on to be foraging for food, it's the last hour before sunset.

Some Factors that Influence the Timing of Feeding Cycles

Because of their extremely wary nature, black bears are sensitive to various weather conditions and other factors that affect their ability to sense or avoid danger.

Winds

Like whitetails, black bears are not likely to be active when winds — steady or gusting — exceed 14 mph. Winds exceeding this velocity cause foliage and branches to make so much noise that it becomes very difficult for black bears to detect approaching danger via their most reliable sense — hearing. Winds 10-14 mph tend to shorten morning and evening daylight feeding hours by 60 minutes or more; winds 6-9 mph shorten them about 30 minutes. Black bears are most active when winds are calm-to-light (5 mph).

Precipitation

Also like whitetails, black bears tend to be very active during periods of fog, mist, drizzle or light rain, winds calm-to-light. Such weather commonly increases the amount of time bears will be active during daylight hours by 1-2 hours, morning or evening. Unlike whitetails, black bears are not particularly bothered by moderate rainfall, as long as winds are calm-to-light. During a moderate rain, feeding cycles tend to fall within more normal hours.

Black bears are most active when winds are calm.

As a rule, black bears will not move during periods of heavy rain. When heavy rain cancels a normal feeding cycle, black bears will be very active as soon as the rain quits or becomes light, winds calm-to-light, whatever the time of day.

Human Activities

Like older whitetails, especially older bucks, black bears of all ages little tolerate unpredictable, short-range human encounters. As human activity increases in an area, fewer bears will be seen during daylight hours, and most that are seen will be young. Human related sounds, such as loud voices and gunshots are more destructive to hunting than human encounters since all bears within hearing are affected.

Are Black Bears Dangerous?

The first burning question among all first-time black bear hunters is, "Are black bears dangerous?" Physically, black bears certainly appear dangerous, obviously having size, strength, speed, fangs and claws that are more than adequate to do serious bodily harm to just about any animal that is human-sized or larger. In fact, they do kill and eat wild animals that are human-sized or larger, though not regularly. Seen in dumps and parks where they receive and expect handouts of food from humans, some even act dangerous, belligerently snatching food from other bears or from humans foolish enough to feed them by hand. Occasionally, some even raid tents, campers, motor vehicles and cabins for food, causing considerable damage and terrorizing humans in the process.

Nevertheless, when encountered at short range by humans in the wilds, black bears generally flee with all possible speed, or sometimes climb trees — even female bears with cubs. Where black bears are common, they are rarely seen by humans. They seem to go out of their way to avoid short-range confrontations with humans. Though humans tend to fear black bears — many humans also flee from near-encounters with all possible speed, or climb trees — the evidence strongly suggests black bears fear humans far more than humans fear black bears. This doubtless accounts for the fact that black bears are capable of living without conflict among humans (unlike grizzlies).

Many insist black bears are "completely harmless." Most of us have seen nature films in which biologists crawl into winter dens to pull wild black bears out by hand in order to weigh them and obtain blood samples. In such films, black bears certainly seem harmless enough — mere Teddy bears. It should be remembered, however, these bears (at least the adults) are in a state of hibernation and/or they are tranquilized.

Actual, documented attacks by black bears on humans are rare — practically unknown. I would guess attacks by rut-crazed, white-tailed bucks are as common (though also relatively rare). Among the hundreds of black bears I have known and hunted during the past five decades — spending considerable time among Minnesota and Ontario black bears (especially within my north-central Minnesota whitetail study area where they are abundant) — I can personally recall only two incidences during which I felt particularly threatened by black bears. In both cases, I admit I provoked the bears. Most black bears I have met at short range that did not immediately move off were either minding their own business — eating blueberries, for example — or they were merely curious about me or my gear, moving off without threat once that curiously was satisfied. On a few occasions, while camping in wilderness areas, I have been visited by obviously hungry bears day and night, but being especially careful to keep everything out of tents that even remotely smells like something good to eat — including toothpaste and deodorant — I have never had a tent damaged by a bear. On the whole, they've been good citizens, interesting and exciting to observe.

Despite all the evidence that suggests black bears are completely harmless, however, I for one would never encourage anyone to feed a wild bear by hand, nor would I ever assure a hunter they are indeed harmless. In fact, I think there is danger in believing black bears are harmless. It encourages inexperienced hunters to be careless with black bears. Baiting, especially, leads to plenty of near-encounters with all sorts black bears, and plenty of opportunities to deliberately threaten or provoke them. Whereas the vast majority of black bears will flee when threatened or provoked by humans, some won't. Some will definitely stand their ground — ready to assert dominance, ready to defend themselves and/or cubs, ready to defend other things important to them or ready to take risks to satisfy hunger.

Tales of hunters who have treated bears as if they are completely harmless — shooting poorly and/or approaching wild bears (wounded or not) without regard for personal safety — always leave me aghast. "One of these days," I always think, "this dude is going to meet the wrong bear." I have met at least two "wrong" bears.

Upon meeting a black bear that does not immediately flee, I have never been able to decide how it will react to whatever I might do. Faced by such a bear, I hesitate to flee, having an eerie feeling flight on my part might trigger a charge. Thus I too hold my ground, challenging such a bear in a manner best understood by bears, engaging it in a war of nerves, bravado and bluff, up to a point, at least until I can decide whether a bear is merely curious, merely bluffing or potentially dangerous.

Initially, I'll merely stare back at a bear that does not flee, standing quietly, erect, facing it squarely. Most wild creatures, including most black bears, are unnerved by the direct gaze of a human. If this doesn't cause the bear to retreat within a minute or so, I'll begin talking quietly to the bear, asking it, for example, "What's your problem, bear?" and then telling it, "I think you ought to leave." The readily-recognized human voice alarms many species of wildlife; even bold black bears. If a bear still refuses to back off, I will then resort to making loud noises, waving my arms, banging on noisy objects and/or hollering, "Git outta here bear!" This is usually enough for most bears. If this doesn't work, there's only one thing left to do — retreat.

When retreating, I back off slowly at first — continually facing the bear — until some distance away. When finally out of sight, I'll either turn and quietly make haste toward distant parts, or retire to a convenient place of safety — a building, a motor vehicle, a canoe out on water or, perhaps, a tree. Once many years ago, I felt it was prudent climb a tree — approached by two running cubs, their obviously irate mother lumbering in their path.

During all the years I have sojourned among wild black bears as a non-hunter, such actions on my part have kept black bears and I from having to square off, hand to paw.

Generally, those who insist black bears are completely harmless are those who do not hunt black bears, and those who insist they are dangerous, or, at least potentially dangerous, are those who are experienced black bear hunters. Obviously, black bears merely being observed by non-threatening humans tend to be gentle animals. Black bears being hunted by life-threatening humans, on the other hand, can demonstrate a hostile nature.

Whereas the vast majority of hunted black bears will turn tail and flee at the least hint of human danger, the hunter should never believe *every* black bear will turn tail and flee. Some black bears have no particular fear of humans — dump and park bears, for example. Such bears readily approach humans, having learned it is easy to obtain food from humans via bold behavior, sometimes using bluffs or threats. At bait sites, dump or park bears look exactly like other bears. When denied or threatened, however, they're more easily provoked.

Baiting inevitably leads to short-range encounters with sows with cubs, and inquisitive cubs can sometimes put themselves into situations in which their mothers might feel they cannot retrieve them from danger without initiating hostile action. Whether an enraged mother bear protecting her cubs is bluffing or not can be difficult to assess, but if there ever was a bear that isn't bluffing, an enraged mother bear will be the one.

Older boars — like grizzlies — sometimes become protective of food caches (bait sites), threatening any other bears that approach. Under the right conditions (heavy wind and/or precipitation, for example), a human could conceivably stumble onto a bear at a bait and be momentarily treated like an intruding bear.

Being at the top of the wild food chain, black bears fear no other creatures in the wilds except more dominant black bears, canines (wolves and domestic dogs) and humans. The largest in any one area do not fear other bears. Being most dominant — accustomed to having things their own way — larger black bears (also females with cubs) often display short tempers when among other bears, inflicting, or threatening to inflict, fearsome punishment at the least bear-type impropriety. This is their way of handling things that do not please them. When provoked by a lesser bear, an enraged dominant bear almost instantly becomes an unflinching engine of destruction. If such a bear is pushed enough by a human (desperately wounded and/or cornered), it may react the only way it knows — giving battle.

While black bears may be harmless otherwise, bear hunters may knowingly or unwittingly create situations in which bears may feel they must defend themselves. When an incautious, foolish or disrespectful hunter approaches one these powerful carnivores, or vice versa, the stage is set for blunders that can lead to serious consequences, made all the more probable by impatience and/or panic on the part of the hunter or the hunted. Though, fortunately, black bears are more cautious, more sensible and more respectful of humans than humans realize, the hunter, at least, should never completely trust black bears. To do so invites inevitable trouble. To illustrate, consider the following accounts of personal encounters with two unforgettable black bears.

The Bear on the Knoll

We — a spirited bunch from Crane Lake, Minnesota — were hunting whitetails on the Canadian side of the border under the direction of resort owner Don Bowser and a tall Indian guide from the nearby Lac La Croix Reservation. My neighbor, Ben Siegly (not a deer hunter), joined us to hunt ruffed grouse. Following a fruitless drive at the east end of Redhorse Lake, we rendezvoused on a rocky beach for shore lunch. It was there that Ben, grinning from ear-to-ear, leaped from his boat saying, "Ken, I found the bear you've been lookin' for. It's on a knoll over on the peninsula I just walked through."

I realized, of course, black bears do not make a habit of lounging long on knolls recently visited by humans. Shortly after lunch, nonetheless, Ben and our Indian guide watched from downwind as I quietly stalked toward the summit of the knoll where the bear was seen. After a minute or two of suspenseful searching, the hair on the back of my neck suddenly arose, finding myself staring into the brown eyes of a tan-muzzled beast of considerable stature glaring through the upraised roots of a fallen cedar only fifteen feet away.

Upon raising my scoped rifle, tree bark began grating loudly behind me. Glancing back, I noted Ben and our guide vigorously scaling separate birch trees, adding little to my rapidly deteriorating confidence at this extraordinary moment. Nonetheless — though my knees were like jelly and quivering uncontrollably — I was determined to maintain a respectable composure, reminding myself (as all bears hunters do) black bears are harmless. This one, though, was clearly not your usual black bear. It did not seem at all intimidated by my near presence. Never before had I seen a wilderness black bear that did not retreat with great speed upon being approached so closely by a human. I began to wonder whether I was the hunter or the hunted.

"Shoot-'im-the-head, shoot-'im-in-the-head," a voice with a Lac La Croix accent hissed behind me. "No," I whispered back. At the moment I was not only thinking I should avoid damaging the bear's skull, but I was recalling some advice once given me by Paul Fox, a Tlingit Indian guide in the Yukon Territory in Canada. "When you shoot a bear," he said, pointing to a pencil drawing of a bear on a brown paper bag flattened on our cook tent table, "you want to kill it dead. Shoot it in the heart. Here. Forget that shoot-'em-in-the-shoulder, take-'em-down business. You don't want to just wound a bear and make it mad. Once a bear gets it's adrenalin up, even if it isn't dangerous, it'll be tough to finish off."

"Okay," I told myself, wondering what part of the bear my scope reticule was currently wavering on, "it's the heart or nothing." Meanwhile, I heard bark grating behind me again, and then some rapid, heavy footsteps. Out of the corner of an eye I caught a glimpse of a tall figure plunging headlong into an adjacent alder swamp. That and the peek-a-boo tactics of a bear that would not run soon brought an end to my patience. Glancing down, I perceived a way to end this stalemate. Reaching slowly, I grasped the end of a three-foot length of rotted log lying at my feet and then launched it spinning over the top of the cedar roots. The nasty woof and the sudden emergence of a 200-pound bruin moving directly toward me was a convincing lesson. "Never again," I admonished myself later, "will I hit a live black bear with a rotten log."

Was it a bone fide charge? I'll never know because I shot the bear and it dropped in its tracks. Having the tendency to embellish matters a tad, many hunters in this situation might've insisted they barely survived a severe mauling or death. Thinking back, whether I just happened to be in the way, whether the bear was a merely making a threatening charge that would have stopped short or whether it was really a charge, the bear had plenty of reason to be mad. As many a hunter is likely to do when a bear is near, I had made a dumb mistake.

The Bear That Came to Breakfast

Ben his wife, Kathy, and my wife and I were canoeing back from a fabulous fishing trip in Quetico Provincial Park. A yellow sunset portending high winds the evening before, we broke camp well before sunrise at the east end of Lac La Croix — a large B.W.C.A body of water on the Minnesota-Ontario border — and made a dash toward Beatty Portage at the west end, hoping to get there before expected whitecaps came up.

Just short of the portage, the lake still calm, we pulled into an offshore island for some much-needed hotcakes and bacon. Being the cook, I served the others first, ladling hotcakes to extended plates as fast as I could. When they finally sat back with finishing cups of coffee, I poured the last of the batter on the smoking grill, my stomach growling in anticipation.

Shortly, Ben arose and disappeared into the thick hazels behind us.

Being a noted prankster, none of us were particularly moved when Ben sprinted past, bellering, "BEAR...BEAR!" When he was chest deep in Lac La Croix, however, we began to believe something was up, especially Kathy who had just finished reading a book about man-eating Glacier Park grizzly bears. "It's right behind you," Ben sputtered. "I think it's a bad one."

"Simmer down," I moaned, calmly flipping my hotcakes. "It's only a black bear. We're not going anywhere until I've eaten my breakfast. Here," I said, handing my spatula to Kathy, "I'll go see what all the excitement is about. This'll probably be another wild goose chase like that night on Sturgeon Lake. Now don't let my hotcakes burn."

Upon rounding the first hazel clump behind the fire, I was brought up short by a large, glowering black bear sitting on its haunches like a dog. Glowering back at it had no effect so I waved my arms and loudly instructed it to leave. That too had no effect, so I grabbed a handful of rocks at a my feet and began pegging them toward the bear (not intending to hit it), shouting some more instructions. Apparently not liking flying rocks, the bear slowly rose and marched off a few yards. Then it turned and began popping snarling teeth, the hair on its neck and hunched back on end. Though I had never heard popping from a bear before, the intent implied by these sounds was obvious enough to me. "Throw everything into the canoes and let's get out of here," I shouted, returning quickly to gather up my cooking gear. "I think this bear is bad!"

As I prodded the hot grill from the fire, the bear rushed into the clearing just to the right of where we had been sitting. I tossed my hotcakes and bacon in the bear's general direction — which it promptly began to devour — and then rushed to a flat rock a short distance away upon which I poured the last of our syrup, figuring this would keep the bear busy until we were safely away. It worked, but not long enough. By the time we had grabbed the last of our gear from the island, the bear was stalking quickly toward us, again popping its teeth. Dumping clattering gear, we rushed out into the water, dragging our canoes behind us. Amidst frantic splashing, we all somehow boarded safely and soon began churning Lac La Croix with paddles, taking grateful leave as our inhospitable host glowered from shore.

To this day, there is no doubt in my mind that this bear was very dangerous, indeed capable of inflicting bodily harm on humans. If we had stayed on that island any longer, I am sure one or more of us would have been injured. This ferocious brute demonstrated absolutely no fear of humans. I shudder to think of what might have happened if had we camped on this island overnight. Upon reporting this incident to B.W.C.A. authorities, this dangerous bear was dispatched.

A friend of mine wounded a large black bear late in the day in Koochiching County some years ago. Aided the next morning by a celebrated bear guide of the region, the bear was at length discovered —

charging from thick cover. The guide dropped it a few feet away with a well-placed shot.

More recently, another hunter in the same region was injured by a wounded black bear.

Antidote for Danger

Heart-shot, the largest and most powerful black bear will drop within 15-20 seconds, posing no threat (especially if the hunter is positioned on an elevated stand platform during that 15-20 seconds). Whether black bears are dangerous or not, then, depends on the hunter. When black bears are hunted as if dangerous — never trusting one to be timid, always respecting a black bear's destructive power and always going for a quickly fatal heart shot — they are extremely unlikely to be dangerous, whatever their size. In fact, they're then as safe to hunt as white-tailed deer.

Portray yourself as being as fearless as you want while relating stories of bear hunting, treat harrowing experiences with black bears as if humorous (as I am want to do), and readily agree with anyone who insists they are harmless, but when hunting black bears, *make no mistakes.* Prepare yourself for the adventure of a lifetime, but *prepare most to give yourself the very best chance to make a perfect heart shot.* Knowing you can make such a shot — every time — you'll be able to remain relatively calm when a bear appears. You'll be able to think clearly; to make proper decisions. With all that going for you, you really won't have much to be concerned about except remaining undetected until you've made that shot.

Chapter 2

Locating Productive Bait/Stand Sites

There are three approaches to locating black bear bait/stand sites: 1) scattergun, 2) let the bears do the walking, or 3) go to the bears. Each has certain advantages and disadvantages.

"Scattergun" Approach

Using the "scattergun" approach, lots of baits — a dozen or more gunny sacks full — are hung in trees (away from other animals) at widely-scattered, randomly-selected sites. Upon checking later, stand sites are prepared at those sites where bears have taken baits.

Though there is merit to this approach, and little or no scouting is required, it has at least five notable disadvantages. First, it takes a lot of bait, time and effort initially. Second, it is unlikely the relative sizes of the bears taking these baits can be determined. Third, larger, more wary black bears will not likely be given enough time to become accustomed to stand site preparations before hunting begins (they need 2-3 weeks). Fourth, baits that were not hit initially are likely to lure bears from established stand sites while hunting is in progress. Fifth, mere gunny sacks full of bait will not "hold" bears more than a day or two.

"Let the Bears do the Walking" Approach

The "Let the Bears do the Walking" approach is predicated on the assumption all bear baits are eventually discovered by bears wherever bears are prevalent, which is generally true. Most hunters who use this approach, however, are thinking more of themselves than bears. Reluctant to transport baits any great distance — or harvested bears — such hunters set up bait sites near roads or trails that can be easily traveled by motor vehicle.

Whether or not bears will be taken at bait sites selected in this manner, depends first on the number of other humans using the nearby roads or trails. Unlike white-tailed deer, black bears are quite wary of motor vehicles and their sounds, and they are very sensitive to the presence of significant numbers of humans on foot. Human movements, when present, are usually concentrated within 1/4-1/2-mile of roads and trails. As a rule, where human intrusions are common within 1/4-1/2-mile of a bait site, only less-experienced, smaller bears will visit the site during legal shooting hours, the site will be visited infrequently, it will be visited during nighttime hours only or it will not be visited at all. Shooting (discharging firearms) in the vicinity of a bait site (the grouse hunting season being open, for example) will keep even less-experienced, smaller bears from appearing during legal hours, if at all.

The speed in which black bears discover bait sites is also a factor. If a randomly selected site is situated where bears do not commonly travel while foraging for food — their fresh signs not evident — regardless of how irresistible a bait may be, it can take several weeks before the site is eventually stumbled upon by one or more bears traveling off-range. The trouble is, black bears are range-orientated animals. They do not travel off-range often. In Minnesota where baiting becomes legal only two weeks before hunting (no pre-hunt baiting allowed in one area), randomly selected bait sites commonly remain untouched by black bears through the opener.

Too often, inexperienced hunters select sites that "look good" to them but "look awful" to black bears. Suffering under the mistaken notion "it is safer to shoot a black bear from a greater distance," many hunters prepare bait/stand sites where a wide, relatively-uncluttered field of view is found. There are at least two serious errors in this: 1) black bears, as a rule, cling to dense cover wherever they go, more especially during daylight hours, and 2) black bears (especially older, experienced bears) will not approach bait sites — places they absolutely know humans occasionally appear — during daylight hours where they cannot remain undetected until very near.

"Go to the Bears" Approach

After you after suffered through enough sessions of seeing only small bears at randomly-selected, easy-to-get-to bait/stand sites, or no bears at all — bears either ignoring your baits or visiting them only at night — and/or after you've struggled and sweated enough while hauling hundreds of pounds of difficult-to-accumulate, perhaps expensive, bait to unproductive sites, you'll inevitably get around to wondering if there might a better way to hunt bears. The "go to the bears" approach is the answer. On the surface, this approach might appear to involve more time and effort, but over the long run it will lead to at least twice as many shooting opportunities per hundred pounds of bait hauled than the random method, or to put it another way, the hunter will likely be successful in less than half the time. The "go to the bears" approach also substantially increases the odds for taking trophy-class bears.

The success of this approach is dependent on bear signs — tracks, droppings, evidences of feeding and bear (scratch) trees — the fresher the signs the better. These signs are found by thoroughly combing (scouting) a prospective hunting area, concentrating on range elements most important to bears — bear trails within thick (difficult for humans to travel) cover, bear feeding areas and water. Bear signs are the only regularly reliable means of determining where black bears spend their time, foraging along favorite routes within individual (exclusive or overlapping) home ranges. Though black bears are incessant and wide travelers, wherever they live there are areas that are regularly visited by bears (under normal circumstances) and others that are rarely visited by bears. Even where black bears are relatively common, at least half of any region scouted will be devoid of bears and bear signs. Bait/stand sites within areas devoid of bear signs are risky — unlikely to be productive — especially when natural bear foods are adequate. Under any circumstances, the greatest number of black bears will be attracted within the shortest period of time to bait sites that are located within areas where bear signs are prevalent. Bear signs are the key to baiting and hunting success.

Of course, when scouting for bear signs, the hunter must not only be able to recognize and properly interpret bear signs, but know where to look for them. These are common failings among bear hunters, especially beginning do-it-yourselfers. Without a reliable guide, it can be difficult to put the stamp of "bear" on most signs made by black bears, much less the stamp of "trophy-class bear." Even where bears are abundant, a beginner can easily spend an entire day afield wandering among countless bear signs — even stepping in them — without identifying a single sign. I've accompanied many a hunter that could not differentiate bear droppings from the droppings of wolves, bucks in rut, moose or humans.

Where to Look for Bear Signs

Wherever black bears are found in North America — north, east, south or west — they all have one thing in common: they prefer the densest woody cover available. They typically cling to forests choked with deep grasses, ferns, shrubs, brush and windfalls within or about wet lowlands or adjacent to streams, rivers and lakes. Within the region I have long hunted, cedar and tamarack swamps are such reliable bear havens that I would not consider preparing a bait/stand site that is not within a stone's throw of one.

Thus, when scouting, though doubtless the bears I hunt spend time in other areas, I head first to game trails within and along the edges of cedar and tamarack swamps where I seldom fail to find bear signs. Bear tracks are particularly discernable in the damp earth of swampside trails (and easy to measure).

Islands or ridges in swamps off mainlands also get my attention. Mature sows typically establish home ranges within larger tracts of highlands, natural fruits, nuts and other foods being most abundant there. Older boars take what is left, including large swamps. Every large bear I have known traveled extensively in swamps, commonly moving from isolated island to island or ridge when foraging for food. Bait sites on swamp islands or ridges are not only more likely to attract larger bears, but they are far less likely to be disturbed by other humans.

Fresh beaver cuttings can be especially fruitful. I'm not sure whether black bears are drawn to beaver ponds because they like to eat beavers or because beaver ponds and their environs are rich in bear-type foods. Perhaps tangles of cuttings make good bear bedding areas. Whatever the reason, our bait/stand sites situated adjacent to fresh beavers cuttings are always productive, often visited by multiple bears. If I knew bears were in an area but could not locate bear signs, I'd set up a bait/stand site next to a beaver pond every time.

How important are reasonably fresh bear signs on or adjacent to well-used game trails coursing through thick cover within or adjacent to wet lowlands and water? The odds are excellent the bear that made any identifiable sign(s) will pass along the same path, or within an easy whiff of it, every 1-4 days.

On nearby highland game trails where soil is dry, even in soft soils bear tracks can be tough to discern. Whenever I find a game trail that is relatively smooth, hard-packed and wide (18+ inches), grasses and other foliage uniformly flattened, I strongly suspect I'm on a bear trail. The large, padded feet — not unlike those of humans — of heavy bears characteristically make regularly-used trails appear flattened. With that thought in mind, along such trails I keep my eyes open for bear droppings and evidences of feeding — freshly-torn, rotten stumps or logs (standing or lying on the ground) or freshly-opened ant hills, for example.

Black bears eat just about everything that has food value. In the wilds they consume prodigious quantities of anything from new-growth vegetation, wild fruits and nuts to wild honey, carrion and anything live they can catch, including ants, insect grubs, spawning fish and

Where beavers are active, there are sure to be black bears.

the newborns of white-tailed deer and moose. Quick to exploit especially nutritious human foods, where accessible, they relish domestic crops such as oats, corn, apples, bee honey, human garbage, fowl and easy-to-catch, young (or dead and discarded) livestock.

Chokecherries

Wilderness landfills (garbage dumps) are especially attractive to black bears, drawing large numbers from considerable distances. I have often observed up to forty bears foraging at several landfills in northern Minnesota. Some hunters, seeking easy harvests, hunt bears in the vicinity of landfills. This I would never do for three reasons: 1) I feel this is

Raspberries

taking unfair advantage of animals made sadly vulnerable, 2) I could never be one bit proud of taking a mere dump bear, whatever its size, and 3) dump bears are not particularly tasty on the table. I would not shoot a bear I would not eat. Unlike dump bears, wilderness "berry-bears" provide among the world's most wonderful steaks — flavorsome beyond compare. I much prefer them over venison steaks. I wouldn't hunt bears within twenty miles of a dump.

Whether hunted during spring or fall, hungry black bears are almost constantly roving in search of food, normally finding mere tidbits here and there. Upon discovering a bountiful source — a shallow stream teeming with spawning fish, a deer carcass, a lush blueberry patch or a hunter's generous bait cache — a bear is likely to remain within the immediate area, bedding nearby until the food source is exhausted.

Mountain Ash.

The most productive of bait/stand sites are those that are situated along the paths more regularly taken by bears while foraging within their home ranges, normally located very near concentrations of natural foods preferred by bears. By September 1st in the region I hunt black bears, wild blueberries, consumed in prodigious quantities earlier, are no longer a significant bear food, and in this region acorns are unknown. In September, our bears key on end-of-the-season (less common) raspberries, strawberries, pincherries, chokecherries, insect grubs found in rotten logs, ants, bog cranberries (when available) and bunchberries (normally very common in the fall). Scarlet bunchberries are most abundant in the shade of larger stands of mature, lowland evergreens. Always noting large numbers of the easily identifiable pits and skins of bunchberries in the droppings of our bears in fall, we accordingly position our baits among concentrations of these wild fruits. Whatever bear foods may be most common in your hunting area, spring or fall, positioning your bait near them will not only insure a quick response when baiting is started, but a longer, more effective period of conditioning (getting bears accustomed to your scents and presence).

Where Dogs Are Used to Hunt Black Bears

While black bears in any one area are being chased by dogs, few bears, if any, will approach bait sites during daylight hours. To assure hunting success via baiting, either establish bait/stand sites in regions where dogs

Wild Rose Hips. *Highbush Cranberries.*

are not commonly used or plan to hunt during periods when dogs are not ordinarily run — mid-week, for example. If dogs are used primarily on weekends, begin hunting on Wednesdays, allowing bears a couple of days to settle down and begin acting "normal" again.

Bunchberries

Recognizing and Interpreting Bear Signs

Except when drawn to unusually rich sources of food, except when breeding and except for sows with cubs, black bears are largely solitary animals that constantly roam over large ranges. For this reason, their signs are are not ordinarily abundant in any one area. Fresh tracks or droppings of any amount are a relatively unusual find. When scouting, then, the hunter must be very attentive, much more so than when scouting for white-tailed deer. As scant as signs might be, the hunter should not be discouraged. It is not necessary to find a lot of bear signs to be a routinely successful bear hunter. The least discovery of a reasonably fresh bear sign can be of enormous value. Because black bears tend to be very habitual in their travels — following the same general paths as they forage for foods — one bone fide bear track (where the bear was not likely alarmed) can be all that is needed to locate an almost-sure-to-be-productive bait/stand site, unless, of course, it is situated where intrusions by other humans are likely (within 1/4-1/2 mile). No single bear sign, then, should be treated lightly. It should be studied closely; gleaned for all it's worth. One fresh sign may be all you'll find, but it can be all you'll need.

Bear Tracks

Bear tracks are so unique — large, almost human-like (hind feet) with obvious claws — that even when indistinct, they can hardly be mistaken for the tracks of anything else.

Long before I discovered experienced bear guides commonly measured bear tracks to estimate bear sizes, I made it a habit of putting a ruler to the tracks I found. After years of measuring the paws of harvested bears, track measurements became a primary tool for keying on trophy-class boars — locating big bear ranges and avoiding sow ranges. Unlike most who measure the widths of fore paws, however, I have always preferred to measure the lengths of hind paws (including claws). Being larger measurements, I believe they are more accurate indexes of bear sizes than widths of fore paws.

I have not yet accumulated enough hind paw measurements to attempt making a graph that accurately correlates track measurements with bear sizes (weights) or ages by sex. I'm not altogether sure it's possible. The trouble is, black bears among similar age groups vary greatly in weight. Some are fat and some are not. Though their paws would be smaller, I'm am sure there are 4-1/2 year-old boars that weigh as much as some 6-1/2 year-old boars. Nonetheless, I routinely use track measurements as a means of estimating approximate bear weights, separating them into six approximate weight groups. The two heaviest groups, having hind paws measuring 8-9 inches or more, are the bears I prefer to hunt. Having estimated the size of a large bear by its hind paw prints, I can't recall ever being particularly wrong. Big black bears — bigness based on skull measurements — generally have big feet. Whereas it has been well noted that some 500-pound black bears have small heads — not being record-book bears — and some 400-pounders have large heads — making them record-book bears — I suspect bears with longer hind paws (larger foot bones) also have larger skulls.

As a rule, average or medium-sized black bears that weigh (live) 180-250 pounds have hind paws that measure 6-7 inches in length (including claws). Bears weighing 300-350 pounds usually have hind paws measuring 8 to 8-1/2 inches in length. Especially-large black bears, those weighing 400-500 pounds or more, typically have hind paws measuring 9 to 9-1/2 inches in length. Any bear that has a hind paw measuring 8-1/2 inches or more deserves serious attention — it may be a Pope and Young or Boone and Crockett bear.

In light of what I have had to say on this subject, do not consider the figures in the following table to be absolute. They are only rough, ballpark figures for well-fed black bears, but I don't think they'll ever steer you far wrong. For sure, they'll tell you when you're hunting a large-to-very-large black bear. I think I can practically guarantee that when you at last see the bear that makes 8-9+ inch-long hind prints, your heart rate will set a new all-time record, and if your heart rate is any measure of a bear, you'll probably be looking at the biggest black bear you ever saw.

A 2-1/2 year-old's paw measures 5 inches.

Length of Hind Prints (in.)	Weight of Bear (lbs.)
4 (or less)	Less than 100 (cub)
5	100-125 (yearling)
6	125-200
7	200-300
8	300-400
9+	400-500+

Bear Droppings

Bear droppings are usually easy to spot because they are typically found in openings, in the middle of well-trampled game trails and often in the center of man-made roads and trails. Black bears are fastidious, it seems, seeking spots with plenty of clearance before squatting to empty their bowels.

The sizes of bear droppings are not a reliable index of the sizes of bears that made them, other than larger masses come from larger bears and smaller masses come from smaller bears. They can establish more than the simple fact that bears are present, however, usually being found on productive-to-hunt bear trails and their contents often revealing what bears are currently eating.

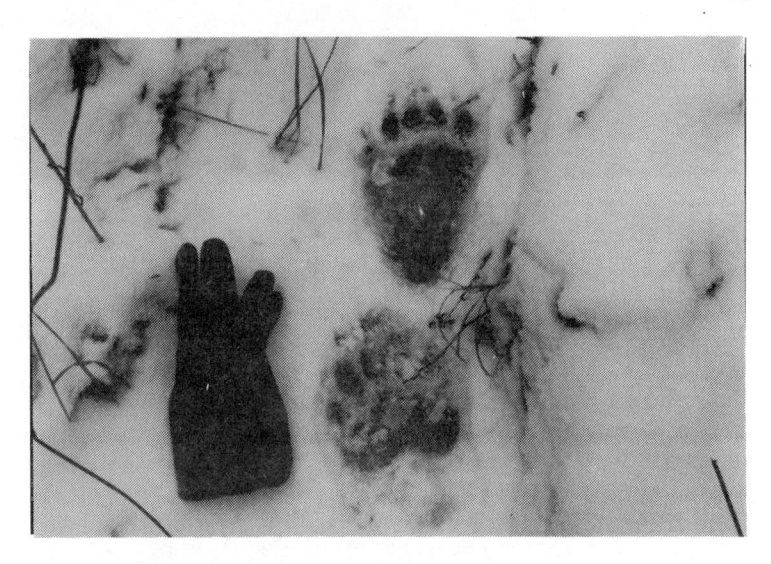

Six-inch long tracks in snow—probably a 200-pounder.

The trouble with identifying bear droppings is, they can vary a great deal in size, shape and appearance, unlike those of most other wild creatures. When feeding on fresh meat, for example, bear droppings tend to be smaller (not much larger than wolf droppings), altogether human-like in appearance, but very dark (almost black). When bear diets are fairly normal (if anything they eat can be considered "normal"), their droppings are larger in diameter and they look like stacks of dark-brown doughnuts lying on edge (in the Old West, cowboys often called doughnuts "bear sign" — see color photo section). When eating carrion (rotten meat) or large quantities of wild fruit, black bears commonly develop diarrhea. Then their stools tend to be light in color (tan, usually) and shaped like domestic cattle droppings — cow pies — only thinner.

Undigested contents of bear droppings can strongly suggest where to scout further and/or where to set up effective bait/stand sites Hair or feathers of a recently eaten creatures in bear droppings may not lead to any noteworthy conclusions, unless the hair is cattle or horse hair or the feathers are those of domestic fowl, but other contents, such as the indigestible parts of wild fruits (berries) or nuts, can be very important clues. Fragments of thin, dark-red (sometimes purplish) skins mean bears are spending time in bogs, eating wild cranberries. Yellow pits with bright scarlet skins mean they're keying on bunchberries — plants of evergreen lowlands. Fragments of acorn shells reveal bears are keying in larger stands of mature oaks. Fish scales mean they're keying on nearby streams. There's no end to what bear droppings might tell you when you can recognize undigestible parts of local flora and fauna. You don't need to find a lot of bear droppings to figure out what most other bears are also currently eating. Black bears are so quick and efficient at exploiting available foods that you can bet whatever one bear is eating, they're all eating.

Signs of Feeding

With some exceptions, clues revealing where bears have been feeding are rarely obvious. Even where recognized bear foods are abundant, it can be difficult to be sure bears have been there. Torn corn stalks accompanied by identifiable tracks or flatted oats accompanied by characteristic droppings may easily add up to "bear," but most of what bears eat are mere scattered tidbits found it places that do not register tracks — consumed quickly in passing with so little ado that even the most experienced eye will fail to notice revealing signs.

This bear has been eating meat, plus chokecherries, judging by the large pits.

Where black bears have spent some time feeding in one place, or where they have been returning to feed repeatedly, the evidence begins to mount, bears notably lacking finesse in their feeding habits. Within dense cover surrounding a newly discovered source of food that takes some time to exhaust, black bears will typically trample new, bear-wide trails. These trails are usually quite obvious, recently lush grasses and foliage appearing well flattened (see color photo section). Not uncommonly, bears will lie flat while feeding (like a dog worrying a bone) or bed adjacent to a food source for extended periods, forming round, nest-like areas of flattened grasses and foliage within patches of dense, standing cover. Bear droppings will be common on new or long-established game trails radiating from such a place. Tuffs of rubbed bear hair and/or claw marks of various widths may be found on nearby tress or bushes. Playful cubs commonly while away the time climbing trees when their mothers feed long in one area. Five-row scratches in tree bark, some three inches wide overall, are solid evidence of the presence of one ore more cubs and an adult sow.

Bunchberry pits and skins suggest bears in the area are foraging in lowland evergreens.

When tempted by fruits on branches high above the ground, black bears can be tough on trees, reaching up and breaking branches or breaking off the tops of smaller trees, leaving them dangling or mangled on the ground.

Upon killing (rare) or discovering the dead carcass of a large animal such as a deer or moose, once satiated, an adult black bear will typically cover or camouflage its remaining prize by loosely scrapping leaves, dead branches and soil over it. This practice is very diagnostic of a bear, especially an older, larger bear. It is probably done to hide the carcass from the usual host of other carrion-eating birds and animals in the area.

Having located several such bear caches over the years, and having observed one large boar at a site where it located a white-tailed doe mortally shot but unrecovered by a hunter, I have discovered some black bears, at least — like grizzlies and wolverines— douse unconsumed carcasses with urine before departing, not uncommonly bedding very near. This may be a means of warning off other bears and carnivores (staking a claim) and/or an attempt to mask the odors of the carcass so it will not be scented by other bears. At any rate, in the absence of grizzlies and wolverines, the stench of urine about a partially eaten carcass — not overpowering by my nose's standards — is diagnostic of "bear."

If a larger carcass is situated in an open or sparsely wooded area, an adult black bear will commonly move it to a more secluded place, either wholly or in sectioned parts. A smaller bear may simply snatch smaller portions and carry them to thick cover to eat in safety, repeating this proc-

Stool common of bears eating decayed meat (bait).

ess until the carcass (or other large food source such as a bait pit) is consumed.

When scouting, the most common and most obvious evidence of bears feeding is typically ignored — torn-open, rotted timber, fallen or standing. This is probably due to the similarity of the chiseling on rotted timber by various woodpeckers. Over a period of time, the work of woodpeckers on a single fallen log or upright tree can become substantial, appearing altogether bear-like in scale or vice versa. Nonetheless, there is a notable difference between the work of bears and woodpeckers, seeking the same repast, mainly insects and insect larvae (sometimes honey — see color photo section). Bears, of course, are limited to rotted timber situated within about six feet of the ground. Most woodpeckers chisel away small bits of rotted wood, mere slivers. Larger pileated or ivory-billed woodpeckers may chisel away larger chunks, up to 2-4 inches in length. Black bears claw or tear away (with teeth) considerably larger chunks. Bears often rip apart rotted stumps and logs, leaving major pieces scattered in disarray or lying in heaps. A careful inspection of probable bear damage to rotted timber will usually reveal claw and fang marks. The fresher such evidence appears, of course, the better. Very old signs of this kind may not be reliable evidence one or more bears is currently foraging in the area.

Bear (Scratch) Trees

There are two kinds of bear trees: 1) those that merely serve as places to scratch itchy skin — a common affliction while bears are shedding winter or summer fur — and 2) those that serve as visual (and perhaps scent) signposts. Sometimes a tree serves both purposes.

The first type of scratch tree is easily identified by black bear hair in varying amounts clinging to ravaged branches or rough bark, or by hair scattered at its base. It may be a larger tree, perhaps rubbed by several bears as they pass during their travels, or it may be a mere, three-foot evergreen. The few I have found had the appearance they were used only once by a single bear. Whereas such a tree likely marks the path more regularly taken by at least one bear, any bear I'm likely see at this spot will be thoroughly inspected for bald patches. I am not overly interested in harvesting a bear that has an incomplete pelt (not very suitable for making into a handsome trophy rug).

The discovery the the second kind of bear tree, is especially exciting to me. A bait/stand near such a tree is likely to be visited by more than one bear, and usually they'll be adult boars, very likely including the largest one in the area. This isn't *always* the case. At one stand near such a bear tree, I saw eight different black bears in a single day, including a sow with twin cubs.

Such a tree is identified by many sets of claw marks in the bark, or in bared wood, at varying heights from the ground (see color photo section). Fang marks may also be present, as well as hair. Each time a local bear passes such a tree, it seems, it will stop to raise up, rub and make claw marks on it as high as it can reach. Boars weighing more than 400 pounds can reach at least 6-12 inches higher than I can reach — an identifying sign of a trophy-class bear. Apparently black bears recognize one another by bear tree claw marks and probably scents. As bears seem to spread their claws as widely as possible when making their individual marks, the widths and heights of claw marks may also be a means of identification. Such scratch trees do not seem to be a means of staking out exclusive home ranges. They seem only to function as a sort of bear newspaper — bears letting others know they are still around, and, perhaps, creating a record that indicates when they last passed the spot. These scratch trees seem to be situated where larger numbers of boars often cross paths as they cruise through overlapping ranges. Perhaps they are a means of avoiding conflict. They may also function as claw-sharpening posts, like posts used by cats.

Dens

It is not only unethical (morally unacceptable; taking unfair advantage of an unusually vulnerable animal) to shoot a bear in a den, but it is illegal. Moreover, it is not effective to locate a bait/stand site near a den. Not all bears hibernate in easily-identified, underground dens, and dens are not regularly situated near paths regularly used when bears are not not hibernating. A stand near a den is unlikely to be productive.

Mapping Bear Signs

Like when preparing to hunt white-tailed deer, all efforts made toward marking the locations of fresh bear signs on an enlarged map of the area are extremely worthwhile. In bear hunting, signs being uncommon, such a map is especially valuable. A carefully made bear sign map will put everything into easy-to-see perspective — likeliest cover, locations of natural bear foods, routes used by foraging bears, best locations for baits, best routes for stand trails and distances to bait/stand sites from roads and trails. When tracks are measured, such a map can even reveal bear numbers and sizes and specific sites for hunting specific bears — trophy-class bears, for example.

Prerequisites of Productive Bait/Stand Sites

Upon locating a likely spot for baiting black bears, a lot of careful thought must go into selecting the exact site. There are a multitude of pitfalls at this point that can easily ruin your chances for success. Before beginning to prepare any bait/stand site, I always sit down and try to anticipate possible problems first — asking myself certain questions and attempting to come up with the best answers. This often means I must scout further in the immediate area. My usual questions are as follows:

Adequate Bear Cover

Is there cover enough here for a bear? Knowing adult black bears are extremely wary of larger openings or areas of sparse cover during daylight hours, I will never waste my time laboriously preparing a bait/stand site where it will be impossible for a bear to remain fairly hidden (at ground level) until within 10-30 yards of my bait. Cover surrounding my bait site must be at least bear-tall and thick during the period when I will be hunting, meaning, I might need to take into account how things will look after deciduous leaves have fallen. Dense grasses or ferns at least 3-4 feet tall and/or thick hazels or alders and windfalls in the shade of mature timber — preferably white cedars, balsams and/or black spruces where I hunt — are ideal. Such cover greatly improves the odds for seeing bears during legal shooting hours. If the spot has favorable bear signs but inadequate cover, I might try to find more suitable cover within 100 yards. Without dense enough cover, I know the spot won't be worth the effort.

Adequate Stand Cover

Is there a tree available that will provide enough cover for my stand? Personal experiences with black bears have convinced me they find it difficult to identify the motionless silhouette of a human in forest cover at a range of fifty yards or more. Within the 10-20 yard range in which I prefer to have my quarry standing when I shoot, however, a bear can very easily identify the silhouette of a hunter — even a motionless hunter perched high in a tree.

When bear hunting, therefore, I insist on using stand trees that provide *optimal* cover at the stand level. I much prefer mature evergreens. Using a chain-on portable stand, I can usually nestle up beneath and in front of thick boughs of a mature evergreen 9-12 feet from the ground without doing much to alter the tree. Ordinarily, upon selecting the right tree I'll only find it necessary to cut away a few branches on the side facing my bait pit. I want thick, natural cover at my back and sides (see color photo section). Between my quarry and I, it depends. As long as I can raise my weapon without interference from branches (while seated), I usually don't need much of a window through the branches in front of me for a clear shot (knowing precisely where the bear will be standing when I fire). As long as I have a fairly solid background of branches to hide my silhouette, however, I do not overly concern myself with having cover between me and a bear. With good personal camo, I have survived many intense gazes by bears within 20 yards without being identified.

On occasion, I have not been able to find a perfect, silhouette-hiding stand tree at the right spot. In some cases I have nailed or tied evergreen boughs to deciduous trees to provide stand covert. As when hunting whitetails, however, whenever major visual changes are necessary to make a stand more effective, these changes should be completed no less than 2-3 weeks before hunting.

Minimal Change

Can I prepare a bait/stand stand at this site without making great changes? By my standards, the "ideal" site includes a heavily-branched, mature evergreen with a 12-inch-plus-diameter trunk (stand tree) situated about 10 yards from an opening about 5 yards in diameter (bait site), no major trees in between and all surrounded by heavy timber and dense undergrowth. The spot will likely have a well-established game trail passing through it and water or a swamp very near.

The site should not require a lot of work with axe or saw, not because I'm lazy, but because older black bears, especially, are wary of places that have been radically altered with axe or saw for a period of at least 2-3 weeks. Cutting a lot of trees or branches 1-1/2 inches or more in diameter in the vicinity of a bear stand is like pitching boulders into the spot where you're planning to fish. The site should remain as natural in appearance as possible.

Undisturbed Bears

Can I get to this site without spooking my quarry? Vital to the success of a bait/stand site is the trail that will be used to get there. Especially when hunting, the 200-yard section of trail nearest the stand must not only allow a silent passage through effective screening cover, but it must

Approacing bait pit amid cover favored by black bears — thick.

not course near where it is likely a baited bear is bedded. Baited bears regularly bed near bait sites.

To answer the above question, the hunter must first answer some other questions, the first being, **where will a baited bear be most likely to bed when not feeding?** The best answer is, the thickest, dry, forest cover available — likely full of windfalls — probably downwind and probably within 200 yards.

Which way will the wind be blowing when hunting? The odds are, somewhere from the southwest to the northwest, prevailing winds being westerly. That means, a baited bear is likely to bed somewhere toward the east and your stand trail should course in from the north, west or south.

Whereas it might appear you will not be able to approach your stand without being detected by airborne human scents, do not allow this concern to alter your thinking. By the time you head to your stand on opening day, every bear that has been feeding at your bait site will have been so conditioned to your scents that they will no longer have an alarming effect.

If suitable bedding cover is not available toward the east — the area in that direction being a tamarack swamp, for example — a baited bear's next best option is, any suitable cover within hearing, likely within 100 yards.

Locating and avoiding an area that fits the bill as a probable bedding area is only the first consideration. Your next question should be, **will I be able to move silently to my stand without being seen?** Ideally, your last 200 yards of trail should course through dense cover. Within this section, you should never cross a clearing. Your trail should be brushed out for silent passage. Ankle-deep mud or water should be bridged with parallel logs. If any of this is impossible, the site will not be effective for bear hunting.

Another question to consider is (see: Chapter 4, "Bait Amounts and Frequency of Baiting"), **will I be able to haul hundreds of pounds of bait over this route?**

Quick Transport of Bear Carcass

Can I move a harvested bear from this site within 4-6 hours? The answer to this question may lie in pre-hunt planning and preparation — lining up the manpower and/or equipment necessary to move a bear quickly to a cooler. If you can't answer "yes" to this question, being too far from the nearest motor vehicle access (or boat or air transportation) or being in an area or situation that otherwise defies transporting a bear out quickly, don't hunt at this site unless you can be certain air temperatures will reach no higher than the upper 30s or low 40s. Well-furred and well-fatted black bears spoil in a remarkably short period of time — within six hours or less — when the temperature is 50°F. or above. No one should hunt black bears without making sure a harvested bear's hide and meat will be used.

Multiple Bait/Stand Sites and Distances Between Stands

Relying on one bait/stand site (selected by an Ontario guide), I have been skunked (no bears visited my bait). Using two or more widely-spaced, personally-selected sites per hunter, my sons, son-in-law and I have never been skunked. Most seasons, we have used 3-5 bait/stand sites per 1-2 hunters. Not uncommonly, at least one of our baits fails to draw bears opening weekend. To make sure every hunter has at least one effective bait, each hunter should prepare two bait/stands sites. One extra for a single hunter or two extras for a group is good insurance.

Multiple stands are especially important when the hunter is determined to take a large bear (boar) only. Bear signs being as scant as they typically are, the hunter may easily end up hunting within the bounds of a sow home range — an area unlikely to be visited by a large boar. To improve the odds — lacking definitive signs — set up bait/stand sites at widely spaced sites at edges of large, wooded swamps. At edges of such swamps, the odds are you will be situated (at worst) at the edges of sow ranges, rather than in their centers. Though large boars are unlikely to intrude deeply into sow ranges, they will approach bait sites at edges of sow ranges.

How far apart should bait/stand sites be? If within a mile of one another, two sites function almost like one. The same bears will either show up at both sites or all at only at one, whichever they feel most secure at. With the exception of adult boars, baits situated more than two miles apart are likely to attract different bears. Because of the great size of their individual ranges, to more successfully bait more than one large boar, baits should be positioned 5-10 miles apart (where signs of very large bears are found, of course).

Bait sites do not need to be strung out along a line several miles long to be optimally effective. We like to position our baits near the corners of a large square, rectangle or pentagon 3-4 square-miles in size, setting up our camp somewhere near the center (1/2-1 mile from each site). This is an efficient way for several hunters to hunt bears together. No one site will be out of earshot and all will be within easy hiking distance of camp.

Ordinarily, the size of the area that should be scouted before baiting, then, is dictated by the number of hunters, the number of stands each decides to use and the sizes of the bears hunted. Where bears are fairly common, two hunters willing to settle for two "average" bears, or one "big" one — using two bait/stand sites each — need only scout and hunt 1–2 square-miles, positioning one bait/stand site, near each corner (where bear signs are found). Each additional hunter in the group — utilizing two sites each — would need an additional adjacent square-mile.

Now then, if you have discovered promising bear signs at a couple of spots, and if there you can answer all of the above questions in the affirmative, you're ready for the next step — preparing bait/stand sites.

Chapter 3

Bait/Stand Site Preparation

Black-Bear-Effective Stands

Having hunted black bears from a great variety of stands — portable and permanent, elevated and surface — I've not only had plenty of opportunity to observe how black bears react to hunters using different kinds of stands, but I've had plenty of opportunity to determine which type of stand best suits bear hunting.

Generally, elevated stands far out-perform ground stands or blinds. Preventing detection via airborne human scents is not likely one of the reasons, however. I believe black bears can detect airborne scents emitted by hunters in trees as readily as they can detect airborne scents of hunters on the ground. Their noses are that much more sensitive than the noses of white-tailed deer. Our latest evidence revealing the amazing sensitivity of a black bear's nose was provided by my son, Dave, last fall.

Dave's Trembling Balsam

Holding out for a chance at a trophy-class bruin, Dave did not bother to raise his bow when an impressive, 5-1/2 foot black bear approached. After circling out of range, the bear turned and moved directly toward Dave's bait, the half-jar portion of honey poured over the logs covering the bait pit foremost in its mind. While lapping honey for some minutes, the bear occasionally glanced up toward Dave. Then it unexpectedly disappeared from view beneath Dave's stand platform. Shortly, Dave's tree began to tremble. Then Dave began to tremble, realizing the bear was climbing. Slowly turning his head to his left, wondering whether he should climb, prepare to defend himself or sit tight, Dave immediately found himself staring from the slots of his camo mask into the questioning eyes of a beast that outweighed him by some 150 pounds, one of its well-clawed paws extended toward the half-empty jar of honey sequestered beneath Dave's canvas stand seat. Though the bruin did not act a bit threatening — more like a kid caught with his hand in a cookie jar — Dave had reason to wonder whether he would someday have the chance to demonstrate how well he had learned a startling new lesson — *never carry food up into a tree stand.* After tensely regarding one another for a minute or so, the bear backed to the ground and without further concern for the leaf-covered creature or the honey in the balsam tree, it began to dine on the less-contested morsels in the bait pit. Though it had obviously identified the honey on Dave's stand platform via airborne scent, this wilderness bear just as obviously failed to identify a well-camouflaged human via scent, even when its nose was only a foot away.

It happens all the time — black bears regularly fail to identify well-camouflaged humans at bait sites, whether hidden on the ground or in a tree. Why? For one reason, bears *expect* to pick up strong human odors at sources of food provided by humans. Secondly, odors at established bait sites — foods in various stages of decay — are typically strong. These strong odors probably mask airborne human odors somewhat — perhaps a great deal. They probably also confound a black bear's ability to recognize where human odors are originating from. Black bears could easily identify hunters perched in trees via scent otherwise.

There are two major reasons elevated stands are most effective: 1) they more or less force a hunter to remain motionless, reducing the risk of being detected by sight or sound, and 2) in an elevated stand a hunter is unlikely to be stumbled upon by the quarry, an inevitable occurrence when hidden on the ground. Of the many types of elevated stands, chain-on or strap-on portables are my personal favorite for bear hunting, being easily placed in mature evergreen trees without having to trim away many boughs.

Essential Bait/Stand Site Elements

An effective black bear bait/stand site is made up of six parts: 1) a well-camouflaged, elevated stand, 2) foods and odors irresistible to bears, 3) a means of keeping other animals and birds from consuming bear baits, 4) aids for sizing-up bears, 5) a clear shooting lane and 6) a secluded stand trail that allows silent passage.

When to Prepare a Bait/Stand Site

As a rule, I never prepare a bear stand site less than two weeks before hunting. With help from my bear hunting crew, this job is routinely completed during the two (sometimes three) days we devote to pre-hunt scouting and initial baiting. Starting out at sunrise each day with a good idea where to search for bear signs (having noted the locations of signs of bears during previous outings) and knowing exactly what to do once we've identified favorable signs, we can usually prepare six or more bait/stand sites over a weekend.

Though I have never hunted in an area where baiting is not allowed until the opener, if I did, I would prepare bait/stand sites in exactly the same manner — two weeks early. Preparing sites early, on opening day I could be certain warier, older bears would not be spooked by any changes I might have made. By keying on bear signs 1/2 mile or more from roads or trails, I'm sure I'd be looking at unsuspecting bruins a matter of 1-2 days, 3-4 days at the most. Beginning baiting as allowed on the opener, I'd hunt no less than four consecutive days.

Stand Site Preparation

Stand Positioning

When preparing a bait/stand site, I like to start with my stand. Upon getting a look at things from the platform level, I not uncommonly find I must change my mind about where the stand or bait should be. Seated at the desired 9-12 foot level, I may discover a certain branch or tree (that should not be cut) will interfere with shooting, my silhouette will not be as well screened as I anticipated, too much cutting will be necessary to provide a clear shot to the bait, or the evening sun will shine directly into my eyes. Sometimes I find it necessary to change the height or angle of my stand and sometimes I'll find it necessary to move to a different tree.

When seated in your stand, you should not face directly toward the spot where your bait will be. There are two reasons.

For one, you'll not be comfortable when taking aim at a bear. Your back and arm muscles will be strained. Almost routinely when hunting black bears over bait, you will be obliged to freeze while aiming (or while at a full-draw with a bow), waiting for the quarry to offer a better shot angle. Upon aiming from an awkward angle, within a minute or two, your strained muscles will be screaming for relief. You may be forced to move while a bear is facing you, or you may be tempted to fire when you shouldn't. Being right-handed, I am most comfortable in my shooting stance when my stand is turned 45 degrees to the right of my target — the bait cache area. Some hunters like to be turned 90 degrees. Be sure to adjust your stand to your own most comfortable position.

For another, when faced squarely toward your bait pit, you will also run the risk of unnerving your quarry because of what your eyes are doing — your head pointed directly toward the bear. Whether it's intuition or something else, most wild creatures will soon sense when another creature is staring at them. When you have a bear within 20 yards, you should never look directly at it until ready to shoot. Keep your eyes pointed somewhere else, observing the bear only via your peripheral vision. When your stand is angled away from the pit, this is much easier to accomplish.

It is difficult to foretell all the stand-related problems that may exist, or how to cure the them, until you've had the chance to sit in your stand, *but discover and cure them you must*. When a black bear finally appears, your stand must enable you to perform as flawlessly as possible. You'll be pitted against one of the very best wild animals there is at detecting humans; also one of the very best there is at escaping when that happens.

Stand Height

A stand platform height of 9-12 feet is just about perfect for bear hunting, I think. At a lower level, not only will you be less likely to spot approaching bears until they are very near — catching you unprepared — but you will likely find it necessary cut a more obvious swath through grasses, shrubs, brush and tree branches in order to insure your bullet or arrow will have a clear path to a bear.

Also, though hesitant to admit it, I prefer a height of no less than 9-12 feet because at this level I know a black bear cannot simply stand up to reach me. Whereas I don't ever expect one will actually stand up and attempt to reach me from the ground, it is a comfort to know it can't be done.

A stand height greater than twelve feet, I think, is foolishness, unless the hunter must climb a bit higher in order to gain silhouette-hiding cover. Greater height does not make a bear hunter more successful, nor does it make a bear hunter safer. If anything, greater height has the opposite effect.

Normally, few experienced stand-hunters are are likely to be careless at greater heights, but black bears characteristically inject so much excitement into hunting that human clumsiness in tree stands is almost a standard part of black bear hunting. Whatever the stand height, a hunter's scrambled nervous system is far more apt to be a danger than a black bear. Even after all my years of bear hunting, I'm still plagued by something akin to physical shock after the fireworks are over. Last September, for example, once I knew the trophy-class bear I shot with my bow was down, I could not trust myself to unhitch my safety strap and climb to the ground for at least ten minutes. Immediately after shooting my first bear many years ago, I lost my footing high in a tree and ended up on the ground with quite a few scrapes and bruises, my clothing in tatters. I was lucky and thankful — thankful the ground was soft, thankful my rifle hadn't misfired, thankful I hadn't climbed higher than twelve feet and thankful the bear lying a few yards away wasn't moving.

A stand height of 9-12 feet is just right for hunting black bears over bait.

Greater height is also unlucky for black bears. It is not often practical, prudent or possible to shoot accurately at a black bear from any great distance, especially when hunting in forested regions over bait. Ordinarily, the quarry will be (or should be) very near when it is time to shoot. The higher a hunter is from the ground, however, the more likely it is that a bear's heavy spine or scapula (the big, flat shoulder bone that angles back over the top of the rib cage) will line up over the quick-kill, heart/lung target area. Moreover, the steeper the angle, the more difficult it is to aim and fire a bow from the recommended sitting position (more about this later). Whatever is used — rifle or bow — a steep-angle-induced spine or scapula hit is practically guaranteed to make your worst fears about bear hunting a reality.

The heaviest arrow from the strongest bow cannot penetrate an adult bear's spine or scapula. A bear with an arrow lodged in its spine or scapula will abruptly disappear. You won't get a second shot. The arrow will probably break off as the bruin barrels through dense brush and then the soft, heavy layer of fat overlying these bones will likely seal the wound. You will soon have virtually no blood sign to follow and little or no chance to recover the wounded bear (a string tracker cannot materially brighten matters). What is worse, the wounded bear will probably die, but not quickly and not without considerable suffering.

A rifleman's mushrooming bullet will likely shatter upon hitting either the spine or scapula. With considerable tissue lying between the heart and the spine or scapula, it is improbable a bear's heart will be damaged with either hit. Hit in the scapula, bullet and bone fragments may damage one or both lungs, but not necessarily with quickly-fatal effect. Hit in the spine, a heavy and/or fast-moving bullet will probably do enough damage to the spinal cord to cause a bear to immediately lose the function of its hind legs. This, however, will not prevent a black bear from dragging itself quickly into nearby cover. In either case, the hunter will need courage and sound shooting instincts to properly finish off the bear.

Strongly of the opinion *prevention is always much better than valor in bear hunting,* I always make very sure I will have a favorable (below-the-scapula) shooting angle when setting up an elevated stand. That's the main reason I never position my stands higher than 9-12 feet.

Stand Camouflage

Being fairly certain black bears are not color-blind, I have long made it a rule to thoroughly cover my portable stands with irregular patterns of flat, camo paints that closely match the stand trees I prefer to use, touching them up annually. My portables are thus nightmarish blends of dark-green, dark-brown and black patterns. To make sure the unnatural odor of fresh paint will not be emitted by my stands when hunting, I paint them at least a month early and hang them outside in a sunny location to weather. Doing this, I seldom find it necessary to add natural cover to my portables to make them less conspicuous.

Stand Comfort and Silence

As older bruins eventually taught us, to be regularly successful at bear hunting, the hunter must be able to sit alert without motion or sound up to 5-6 hours straight. It isn't easy. Either you (especially the part of your body you sit on) must be well-conditioned or your stand must be fairly comfortable. If your stand isn't comfortable enough to allow you to sit motionless that long, fix it or get new one. Whatever you might do to make your stand more comfortable — add a cushion, for example — be sure you do not add a noisy fabric. Some fabrics are particularly noisy when rubbed. Make sure your stand does not squeak, rattle, snap or grate as you shift your weight. Subdue such sounds with padding, nuts and bolts, camo tape or whatever else might be necessary.

Though a subject that will be covered in greater detail in a later chapter, it should be mentioned here that you must be comfortable while shooting from a sitting position. When bear hunting, you must not only remain seated while waiting for a bear to appear, but whether using a gun or bow, you should never stand up to shoot. Whether purchasing a new portable or constructing a permanent stand at a bait site, make sure no part of your stand will interfere with shooting while sitting. Well before hunting begins, rehearse all the motions of shooting while seated in your stand, making certain it can be done without causing the least sound.

Stand Safety

Though widely recommended, a lot of deer hunters (like a lot of people who drive cars) do not hitch up safety belts when when seated in elevated stands. Little wonder so many hunters are injured as a result of falls from elevated stands each season. One hunter I personally know broke a hip and laid abed in a body cast for six months as a result of such a fall. He still doesn't use a safety belt. Many falls are attributable to fatigue (falling asleep) and "buck fever." Fatigue is an undeniable part of sitting motionless 5-6 hours in a tree stand, and mere "buck fever" is nothing compared to "bear fever." No bear is worth taking the risk of being injured or killed for lack of a safety belt. Never hunt bears without one.

Bait Site Preparation

My first experiences with baiting took place in Ontario, Canada. The baits I used were set out for bears by professional guides. Some baits were merely dumped on the ground and others were placed in gunny sacks tied to trees at strategic (or not so strategic) sites. However it was done, the amount and variety of baits used were limited, replaced as needed whenever bears or other animals and birds cleaned them up. In some cases, crows, ravens and Canada jays consumed baits so quickly that they hardly had the chance to attract bears. Often, too, when a bear did hit such a bait, it would consume the entire amount during a single visit and then not return again for some time. Sitting for long hours among hordes of ravenous mosquitoes near such baits, and having paid a lot of hard-earned money for the privilege, I began to consider how I might personally improve matters, given the opportunity.

When the opportunity came, though a first-time do-it-yourselfer, I had some definite improvements in mind. My baits, I decided, should 1) be generous enough to keep bears returning for several days, 2) be protected from other animals and birds, 3) attract bears from considerable distances and 4) include a means of accurately sizing-up bears. These goals, plus the restrictions imposed by Minnesota baiting regulations, became overriding guidelines that still influence how we prepare our bait sites.

The steps we follow are as follows:

1. Select a well-drained site within 10-20 yards of the stand. One of the real advantages of baiting is, you can place your bait exactly where you want your quarry to be standing when you take your shot. You can thus not only put your bait where the least amount of preparation is required (always best) to assure an open shot, but you can position the bear within the range in which you can be absolutely certain of hitting your target — the bear's heart. Whether using a bow or firearm, place your bait at the distance from which you can shoot every practice arrow or bullet into a 1-inch circle while sitting during practice (see "How to Shoot Black Bears"). However accurate you might be during practice, do not place your bait more than 20 yards or less than 10 yards from your stand whether using a firearm or a bow.

The bait site should be well-drained because bait immersed in water is not very effective. A gentle slope in sandy or gravelly soil or rocks makes an ideal bait site.

2. Dig a pit about three-feet in diameter and two feet deep. Three considerations led us to the decision to use pits dug into the ground for bear bait presentation: 1) I wanted to use more bait than could be contained in a gunny sack, some of which would be semi-liquid, 2) Minnesota regulations prohibited the use of non-biodegradable materials at a bear bait site, making metal containers such as oil drums prohibitive, and 3) I wanted to be able to protect our baits from other animals and birds, at least until black bears were on the scene. Ground pits about three feet in diameter by two feet deep covered by heavy logs fit the bill admirably (see color photo section). Occasionally, we make use of natural depressions.

Where water drainage looks like it will be a problem, we'll either dig a narrow trench leading from the downhill side of a pit, dig the pit deeper and then line it with chunks or wood or rocks or build a crib on the surface using heavy logs or rocks to securely contain the bait.

3. Spread soil loosely about the pit. As we dig, we create an apron of loose soil 4-5 feet wide surrounding our bait pits. This soil provides us with a means of assessing bear tracks. By measuring the lengths of individual hind prints, we can determine sizes and numbers of bears visiting a pit (see color photo section). When bears are on a bait, this soil will quickly become hard-packed, making track identification difficult. Each time we bait, therefore, we stir the soil of our aprons with a stick, shovel or rake.

4. Upon adding bait, tightly cover the pit with heavy, six-foot logs. Larger quantities of baits provided regularly over a 2-3 (or more) week period represent a considerable investment in time, effort and money. When our pits are tightly covered with heavy, 100-pound-plus logs, none but powerful black bears can reach our baits.

Apron of loose soil surrounds bait pit.

Invariably, while preparing a bait/stand site, we'll find at least 1-2 large windfalls or standing dead trees nearby, the heavy trunks of which we cut into measured, six-foot-long sections. We use logs that are usually heavy enough to require two men to carry them. Laid side-by-side, 5-6 of such logs will completely cover one of our bait pits (see color photo section).

Besides protecting baits, these logs serve two other other important functions. For one, when laid side-by-side at a right angle to a line between the stand and bait pit, these logs regularly cause black bears to stand broadside — improving the odds for perfect shot angles. Medium-to-large bears tend to stand parallel to these logs when opening a pit, rolling or flinging them to one side with a fore paw. Black bears will usually move only 2-3 of these logs when opening a pit, and then they seem to like to stand on top of the undisturbed logs, facing one end or the other.

These logs also make efficient bear measuring devices. Without them, it is very easy to misjudge the size of a bear. To illustrate, consider Dave's first bear:

Loose soil about pits enables us to determine sizes and numbers of visiting bears.

Dave's First Bear

Time was running out. We were going to have to break camp right after sundown — in about an hour — in order to get my bear to a locker plant before it began spoiling. My son, Dave, understood that. Sure, we could try again another weekend, but this was Dave's first bear hunt, one he had looked forward to for so many years. The outlook was not favorable, however. Bears were unaccountably scarce. Thus far (our second day of hunting), we had only seen three — one Dave spotted while on the way to his stand opening day, the small bear I turned down opening day and the one I shot five hours earlier.

As cool shadows lengthened across the spring-fed pond on our left, a bear suddenly emerged from the thick hazels on the far shore. "It looks good," I whispered excitedly.

We were in a rush to get this bruin to a butcher.

The bear immediately turned and disappeared.

"My gosh," I murmured, "what made it to do *that*?"

"I think it heard your voice, Dad," Dave whispered, a crestfallen expression on his face. "It couldn't have seen or smelled us."

"That's hard to believe," I replied softly. "At that distance, a good 75 yards, a whitetail would never have heard a whisper like that. Wow, if black bears can hear *that* well, we've got some serious thinking to do about how we hunt them.

"Sorry," I added. "It looked like a nice bear too. It's head was certainly small in proportion to its body, its ears looked small and widely spaced, its neck was thick, rump wide and its belly hung pretty low between its hind legs. That had to be a *big bear*."

Some thirty minutes later, barely fifteen minutes before sunset, the same bear reappeared at the same spot As it cautiously rounded the pond toward us, it stopped every few steps to listen and stare in our direction. Apparently it had not been absolutely sure of what it had heard earlier. Given a second chance, we were not about to make the same mistake.

Ten minutes later, the bruin stood broadside on the logs over the pit. At the roar of Dave's rifle, the bear raced toward the pond, ran into a tree and fell lifeless six yards from the pit.

"Wow, what a shot!" I bellered, slapping my beaming son on the back.

"Not too big is it , Dad," Dave presently noted. "It's not near as big as it looked, but I'll sure take it. It's a beautiful bear.

"Let's take those pictures you wanted."

Anxious to prevent this sort of error from ever occurring again, we began cutting six-foot-long poles, nailing them to stakes a yard or two beyond our pits to use as measuring sticks. Visiting bruins, however, seemed to delight in destroying them, either rolling heavy pit logs over them, or tearing them loose and swatting them around. Finally, I seized upon the idea of cutting our pit logs the proper lengths. Nowadays, we always have a ready and infallible means of sizing-up bears.

Thus we prepare our 15-foot-diameter bait sites. They're simple, inexpensive and marvelously efficient; not at all intimidating to the wariest of bears.

Shooting Lane Preparation

After preparing your stand and bait pit, do not cut down everything in between to create an open shooting lane. Making a 15-foot–diameter clearing about your bait pit is about as far as you should go. The wider and more obvious the path between your stand and bait pit, the more reluctant bears will be to approach your pit during daylight hours.

A wide and obvious path will also have the tendency to attract a bear's attention to you — like a wide sidewalk leading to the front door of a house. Keep in mind, being off the ground in no way guarantees you will not be spotted by a bear. Being tree climbers, bears frequently look up into trees. Perhaps at bait sites they expect to spot other bears in trees. The tendency to frequently look up into trees may also reflect a black bear's penchant for honey. Upon detecting the smell of honey at a bait site, a bear probably expects to spot a wasp's nest dangling from a branch overhead, or bee's swarming about an opening in a hollow tree trunk.

Strive always to keep your stand tree, your stand and yourself insignificant in the landscape, separated by natural foliage and trees, as much as possible, from the bait site.

While seated in your stand, direct a partner or two on the ground. Have them trim from your shooting path only what is necessary. Branches and the tops of younger trees nearer your stand should be cut neatly, high from the ground. A tree trimmer with a saw blade and shears at the end of a long, telescoping handle is a handy tool for this job. Trees more than an inch in diameter should be preserved, trimming away only necessary branches. Large trees in the immediate vicinity of a bait/stand site should never be cut down. Since you know exactly where your quarry will be when you take aim, your shooting lane need only be as wide as your bait pit clearing at its far end. At your end, all you'll need is a window about three-foot square. Cut branches should be carried from the immediate area.

Dave's first black bear.

Stand Trail Preparation

When bear hunting, the trail to your stand serves three important functions: 1) its a route for hauling in baits, 2) it's a route for sneaking undetected to your stand when hunting and 3) it's a route for hauling out a bear carcass. The first and third functions call for an easy-to-travel path and the shortest possible distance. The second demands silence and good screening cover, especially within the 200-yard section nearest the stand, the stand trail avoiding probable, nearby bedding areas of baited bears.

Because wild black bears are much warier of motorized vehicles than white-tailed deer, the use of all-terrain-vehicles for transporting baits directly to bait sites not recommended. For best results, the last 200 yards (more is better) should be limited to foot-travel-only.

By far the most convenient and effortless way to transport heavy quantities of baits through forest cover is to load it into a toboggan-like, plastic sled (the type commonly sold in children's toy stores) and pull it in. Backpacking or hand-carrying bait in sacks or buckets is not only back-breaking work, but it tends to severely limit the amount of bait that will be used. On a short rope harness looped around the waist, a plastic sled loaded with 150 pounds of bait will slide easily over soil, ground cover and lesser logs, requiring far less effort than carrying 50 pounds of bait by hand.

Sled full of bait grooming a stand trail.

Whatever method is used, to accommodate bait hauling and bear dragging, the bear hunter's stand trail should be cleared of brush and fallen timber — about 30 inches wide. Even when making use of well-established game trails, the bear hunter will usually find plenty of need for a chainsaw and light axe. In low, wet areas, it may be necessary to lay log walkways — parallel logs nailed together with short lengths of small-diameter tree limbs. Once cleared, with each succeeding baiting the trail will become easier and faster to negotiate, and quieter underfoot.

Bait Storage

If you are planning to camp within the area in which you will hunt black bears, one other another question should be considered: **where will you store reserve bait?**

Once your bears have figured out where the bait is coming from — who is responsible — and once they also discover the familiar odors of bait in your camp, some bears may not wait for you to deliver it to their accustomed dining spots. One night, you're very likely to have a hungry bear in camp. It is foolhardy to store bait in a motor vehicle, trailer, camper or tent. Any bear that can effortlessly fling 100-pound-plus logs from a bait pit can easily force its way into any camp storage place it can reach. If you are planning to store bait in camp, put it in a place bears can't reach. If you don't have such a place, build one.

Between 3-4 adjacent trees, well away from other trees and a short distance from camp, construct a platform 10-12 feet from the ground. To do this, you'll need a portable ladder. Either bring one from home or make one from natural materials (trees). Beneath your platform, trim branches from tree trunks. Then nail bands of 24-inch-wide sheet metal completely around all platform trees, the lower edges at least eight feet above the ground. When not in use, keep your ladder leaning somewhere else (see color photo section).

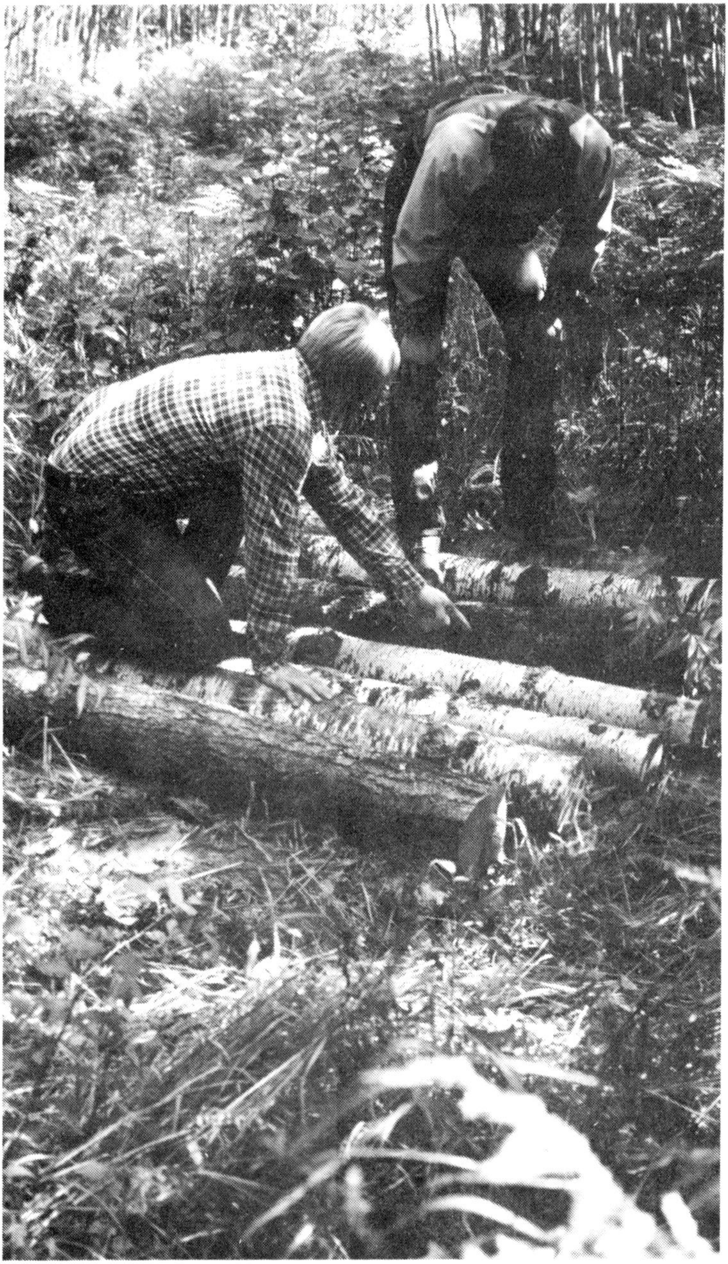

Chapter 4

Baits and Baiting Tactics

On the surface, baiting black bears seems simple enough, and often it is. Many first-time, do-it-yourselfers have very successfully baited bears. Any hunter who has baited black bears over a number of seasons, however, inevitably realizes there is much more to baiting and hunting black bears than simply dumping food in the woods and waiting for a bear to appear. In time, the failure to attract bears during legal shooting hours and/or the failure to attract larger bears leads to experimentation. Thus has evolved a myriad of personalized bear baiting methods all across North America, some of the best of which are closely-guarded secrets of professional guides who make a living baiting bears.

Actually, I think just about anything works, but some baits and techniques truly are more effective than others. Also, some work better in some areas than others, probably due to the fact that while black bears eat just about everything, their diets vary greatly from from region to region. Also, baiting regulations vary greatly from region to region, causing hunters to rely on baits or techniques completely foreign to hunters in other regions.

Following a relatively easy round of taking small-to-medium-sized black bears, my sons, son-in-law and I began to turn our attention to big bears — the largely-unseen, 400-500+ pound phantoms we knew we had in our favorite hunting area. Having been a serious naturalist of whitetailed deer over the past twenty-one years, also observing many, unsuspecting black bears during that period, I have developed a respect bordering on "awe" for the superior intelligence routinely demonstrated by older animals of either species. Almost everything they do has one or more very good reasons, usually having something to do with survival. Understanding these reasons leads to black bear predictability, and thence to vulnerability. As we became more familiar with black bears, we began to tie our baits and baiting techniques to predictable behavior (survival) patterns of older, larger bears. Thus evolved our currently-used baits and baiting tactics, long proven regularly successful for attracting large-to-very-large boars.

Being fully aware of the fact that the baits and tactics I personally use today may vary greatly from those used successfully by others, and also being aware of the fact that what I recommend may not be legal in other states or Canadian provinces, it is therefore not my intention to present "strict" guidelines for baits and baiting tactics. Rather, it is my intention to stress "reasons" for using specific baits and baiting tactics, leaving the way open to make improvements or modifications within legal or regionally-successful black bear baiting guidelines.

Elements of Effectiveness

Today, our pits and their environs emit the odors of twelve different baits, sometimes more. These baits can be divided into five basic groups: 1) meats, 2) vegetables, 3) fruits, 4) sweets and 5) cooking greases and oils. The number, variety and quantity of baits we use provide several important advantages.

Competitive

Our baits perform well against stiff competition. Natural foods regularly consumed by bears are often abundant when baiting begins. The bears we want to attract are probably accustomed to finding a great variety of natural foods throughout their ranges. They will probably be fat, well-fed and content.

Dave and John with "easy bears."

At the moment one lifts it head to consider the odors emanating from one of our bait pits, the bear may be standing in the midst of abundant natural food. The odors from a bait pit, therefore, must greatly impress the bear. Via airborne scents alone, the bear must become convinced it has discovered a source of food that is far superior to any within its range. The offering must be so irresistible that a bear will readily abandon natural foods and travel out of its way to the bait pit. Because a bear may consider some baits to be no more appealing than whatever natural food it may be currently feeding on, a great enough variety must be provided to insure at least some baits will outclass available natural foods.

Holding Power

It will take a bear 3-4 days to consume the quantity we provide. Not able to consume it all in one visit, a bear will remain near when not feeding and it will return regularly until the food is exhausted.

Latent Attraction

Even after bait is exhausted, bears will return regularly. Rich food odors emanating from the soil lining the bait pit, and from bones, will regularly draw bears an additional day or two. Over a considerable period after that, bears will go out of their way to check our bait pits once every 1-4 days — the time period depending on the size of a bear's range.

Mask Human Odors

Our baits mask human odors (or confuse bear noses). Because of the great variety of strong odors emanating from our bait pits — foods in various stages of decay — a bear's sense of smell will be so handicapped that it will be unlikely to distinguish odors originating directly from a human hidden in a tree above from those human odors that are normally mingled with bait odors at the bait site while a human is not present. Human odors are a normal part of the total package. Thus, even though a bear may indeed smell a human hidden in an adjacent tree when at the pit, it will ignore human odors unless the human makes its presence known via an obvious silhouette, a rapid motion or an unnatural sound.

Long-Range Attraction

Our baits draw bears from considerable distances. We utilize a combination of potent airborne and trail scents that can effectively attract bears from distances of 5-10 miles.

Recommended Baits

Meats

Meats are the bread and butter of our bait pits, comprising half or more of the total weight of baits used. We normally add 75-100 pounds of meat to each pit at each baiting. Most of this meat is made up of of **fresh beef scraps, bones and suet,** purchased ($.10 per lb.) at a local butcher shop. Occasionally the butcher will include fresh **chicken scraps** and/or **fish parts,** which is fine. About five pounds of the meat we provide per baiting is **dried dog food.** When I have fish (old or freezer-burned) available, I divide this notably aromatic meat among my pits as well. All **table scraps** (especially meats) from home also regularly make their way to my pits.

Black bears are gluttonous carnivores, unable to resist golden opportunities to consume easy-to-obtain meats (normally infrequent). The odors of meats have tremendous drawing power, and once a bear has found a bait pit, meat will keep a bear coming back, even 1-2 days after the meat is exhausted. Though the actual amount of red meat in the beef scraps, bones and suet we provide is small, black bears don't seem to mind. They treat everything that smells like meat as if it's 100% red meat, consuming every edible bit, except the heaviest of bones. Heavy bones are not wasted, however. Black bears, like dogs, seem to enjoy bones. They'll keep returning to a pit just for the pleasure of gnawing on them. What is great about this bait is, it can be provided in large quantities without great cost.

Any kind of meat would probably be as effective, including pork, but fresh pork (prohibited in Minnesota) should not be used as a bear bait. Though bears love it, uncooked pork is a source of parasitic trichina worms which infest digestive tracts, encyst in muscles (larvae) and cause other ill effects in black bears, as well as humans. It is not wise to introduce trichinosis into a wild bear population.

It is popular to believe "the riper the meat, the more effective it is as bear bait." Sure, black bears devour putrid carrion, and sure, when they're hungry enough, they'll even eat meat so decomposed that it's liquified and alive with squirming maggots, but when given the choice, every wild black bear I have ever known has demonstrated a marked preference for *fresh* meats. I have repeatedly seen black bears pass up very ripe meat in favor of fresh meat. I've had bait pits containing putrid meat ignored up to three weeks (where bears were very abundant). As strong as rotten meats characteristically smell, I believe fresh meats draw bears just as far, only more quickly and more often.

I therefore do my best to provide bears with the freshest meats possible. If the butcher can't do it, or unless we head immediately to our bait pits, I divide meat into 75-pound portions (the right amount for one bait pit) and store it in a freezer until used. Our bears seem to appreciate this consideration.

Dried dog food made our list of top-twelve bear baits by virtue of the fearless determination nocturnal bears have demonstrated when pilfering dog food from outside dog dishes in our camps. They've done it often enough, even while furious dogs barked at them from inside our tents, to make me a firm believer in the efficacy of dog food. Though dried dog food has little odor, it has the advantage of remaining unspoiled longer than almost any other foods we use (at least until a day or two after being soaked by rain).

Vegetables and Grain

Though doubtless there are a great number of vegetables — fresh or cooked — that can effectively attract black bears, the only one we currently use is **fresh sweet corn on the cob**, husks intact to preserve freshness. The last two bears we have taken were bow-shot while they were intently nibbling sweet corn. Needless to say, I would never bait a pit without placing at least 6-12 cobs of sweet corn atop the heap.

Though I do not use it, **fermented grain** — highly aromatic — is truly a *first-class* bear bait. If I hunted in an area where types and amounts of bait were severely restricted, or where I could not use meat scraps or honey, the bulk of the bait I would use would certainly be fermented grain.

Fermented grain is easy to prepare. Into a clean 55-gallon barrel (or garbage can), dump 10 gallons of corn, barley, wheat or oats, 5 gallons of water and 10 pounds of sugar. Stir well, cover and wait one week (Nolan and Ertz 1988). Bears will love it.

Fruits

Black bears relish all kinds of fruits, especially fruits that are sweet and aromatic, whether they are ripe, over-ripe and/or fermented. When hunting in the fall, I make good use of wormy, **backyard fruits** (which pleases neighbors). **Apples, crabapples** and **plums** decomposing on the ground are gathered first. Frost-bitten, fermented fruits — heady in odor — are especially prized by black bears. When abundant, 2-1/2 to 5 gallons of such fruits go into each of our pits at each baiting.

Our coup de grace of fruit offerings is **watermelon.** When honey is not provided at a pit, watermelon is usually the first bait taken by visiting black bears — they like it that much. Watermelon is also an excellent scent-type lure, its sweet, intense odor increasing in strength as the fruit ages. Generally, we add 1/2-watermelon to each pit at each baiting, shattering each half into smaller chunks by flinging it against a log lying over an opened pit. Smashed watermelon has a much greater surface area, releasing a correspondingly greater volume of odor.

Sweets

As commonly portrayed in children's tales, black bears have an insatiable sweet tooth. Ordinarily, however, other than less-sweet wild fruits — usually tart, bland or difficult to obtain in quantity — about the only significant sweet bears are likely to enjoy in the wilds is honey. Upon discovering a source of of this sugary treat — a nest guarded by fierce bees or wasps — a black bear will recklessly climb to a precarious perch, spend hours frantically ripping open a hollow tree and/or willingly endure countless stings about its vulnerable eyes, nose and lips for one mere taste of bee or wasp-infested honey.

Honey is the premier of bear baits. Unfortunately it is expensive (prohibited in Wisconsin). My sons, son-in-law and I use honey sparingly, reserving it for use only when hunting. We usually dispense about one cup at our bait/stand sites daily. This amount is as effective as a pint or more (revealed by comparative testing). To get the most from a cup of honey, rather than dump it into a bait pit, we either dribble it widely over the logs on top or spread it over the rough bark of a mature tree adjacent to our bait pits (never on stand trees, of course). In special cases, we also boil or burn honey (more about this later).

Fruit preserves make up the bulk of the sweets we provide at bait pits. Each time we bait, we routinely add 50 pounds of preserves — preferably strawberry, raspberry, blueberry or mixed fruits, honey sometimes blended in. Apricot and other preserves made from fruits unknown to the bears we've baited have clearly not been as effective. The volume of fruit preserves we use would cost a fortune if purchased at the local grocery store. However, my son-in-law — in a business closely allied with the wholesale food business — always seems to be able to come up with plenty of 50-pound containers of preserves, out-dated, unmarketable and cheap. Though we've never had reason to use lesser volumes of preserves, like honey, I suspect smaller volumes would be as effective.

We do not currently utilize other forms of sweets, but we have and we would again if the preserves we now use weren't available. **Molasses** (or **maple syrup**) would certainly be high on our list; also **stale pastries**, available at little or no cost from businesses that manufacture and/or sell pastries. We'd also use all the **stale candies** we could lay our hands on, especially soft or sticky candies which tend to be more aromatic than hard candies. **Chocolate** and **licorice** are among the best.

With a little creative thought and scrounging, there's no end to the possibilities for obtaining sweets at little or no cost. Though not otherwise considered a "hunting skill," skill in accumulating lots of cheap sweets is very important to success in hunting black bears.

Cooking Oils and Greases

Though black bears would lap up all the used cooking oil and grease we might provide, we use them primarily as scent-type lures.

With each "initial" baiting we pour and stir about 2-1/2 gallons of well-used cooking oil (obtained from a local restaurant) into the apron of loose soil that surrounds our bait pits. In addition to acting as a very potent airborne bear lure, pit apron cooking oil soon also becomes a long-range, trail-scent lure. How? From the moment a bear steps onto the oil-laden apron surrounding one of our pits, wherever it travels, it will lay down a potent cooking-oil scent trail that will lead other bears unerringly to our pit. This remarkable technique is made particularly effective by a boar's tendency to travel where other boars travel. Cooking oil used in this manner draws more bears more quickly that any method we've ever tried.

Leaving nothing to chance, we also create potent man-made scent trails that intercept and draw bears to our pits. Using **religiously-saved, semi-solid, meat greases** — primarily highly-aromatic **bacon grease** — **we paint (using a stiff brush) dollops of grease into rough bark about two feet from the ground on trunks of mature trees spaced**

10-20 yards apart adjacent to major deer trails out to 1/2-mile from our pits in at least two directions. Painting grease as we do, birds and animals cannot quickly consume it, and it is protected from rain, lengthening considerably its period of effectiveness. Prevailing winds normally being from the west, we make our grease trails along trails coursing roughly north and south. This creates enormous downwind scent vectors that also intercept bears moving parallel to our grease trails.

There are other aromatic substances that are used by bear hunters in the same way. One that comes to mind is oil of anise. Having never tried it, I cannot pass judgment on it, but I understand it is effective.

Another is bear urine. The few times I've tried one commercially bottled bear urine, not only did bears fail to return to bait pits that were regularly visited before, but at least two bears I saw in the vicinity acted as if somewhat alarmed — uncharacteristic of earlier visits. Though I can't be certain, I have the feeling bear urine — sometimes (perhaps always) sprayed on food caches by large, dominant bears — can intimidate lesser bears enough to keep them away. One urine sample purported to contain sow-in-heat pheromone had no attractiveness to other bears. Perhaps the pheromone had deteriorated.

Baiting Tactics

By and large, the relative success of baiting reflects the degree of understanding and attention paid to four crucial elements: 1) the manner in which baits are provided, 2) when baits are provided 3) how much bait is provided and 4) how often baits are provided. These elements have everything to do with how many bears will be successfully baited, how quickly, how long, their sizes (ages), whether they appear during legal shooting hours or not and the amount of time that must be spent hunting before an acceptable bear is harvested.

How to Provide Baits

"Noise" is the key. Hunters should be noisy while hauling baits to bait sites, noisy while depositing baits at bait sites, and noisy while departing from bait sites — noisy enough to make sure all bears within 1/2-mile understand what is happening.

For most hunters, making adequate noise is easy. While in the wilds, most humans break enough dry branches underfoot, stumble, stomp, drag feet, sneeze, cough, whistle and talk out loud enough to make it very easy for every creature within 1/2-mile to identify them. Though contrary to recommended hunting procedure otherwise, when baiting, the hunter should freely indulge in these common errors —though not unduly — making an extra effort while it is windy, rainy or when the ground is wet and/or quiet underfoot. There are two important reasons for being noisy.

First, it's a matter of safety. While baiting, every attempt should be made to avoid sudden, unexpected, short-range encounters with intently-feeding bears at bait/stand sites. Such encounters may occur during any hour of the day. This precaution can be particularly important when the bear that might be stumbled upon happens to be a sow accompanied by cubs.

Second, it's a matter of sound black bear hunting psychology (conditioning).

A black bear should never be given a reason to believe "unexpected, short-range encounters with feared humans are likely at a bait pit." Once an adult bear has experienced an unexpected encounter — forced to flee in panic — it will not be inclined to return to that site after the period during which it knows humans are likely to be afoot, mainly during daylight hours. It may not return at all.

Make sure, then, that bears in the vicinity of your bait site know via sounds exactly when you are approaching with bait, giving them plenty of opportunity to avoid a short-range encounter without alarm or haste. Make sure they also know when you are leaving so they will not make the mistake of returning too soon. As long as nearby bears can keep track of your movements via your sounds, they will feel secure in the vicinity of your bait pit. If you make a habit of moving silently, appearing unexpectedly, while baiting, none will feel secure near your bait pit, except, perhaps, at night.

The "noisy human" approach sets up the wariest black bear for an easy kill. Even though human scent may be regularly discernable, the quarry that is conditioned to believe it is nonetheless completely safe from any sudden, unexpected, short-range encounter with a feared human at a bait site will not only ignore human odors there, but it will feel free to approach the site at any time during daylight hours (other than when you are baiting) — even a super-cautious, trophy-class black bear which may otherwise feed only at night. Made secure by your actions, and your time table (more about this later), such a bear may decide it doesn't need to wait until it is dark (safe) to approach your pit.

Noisy baiting makes possible the following series of events (in this case using "the two-man, baiting-hunting system"): 1) bear hears noisy, scent-laden humans approach with customary food, 2) bear hears noisy, scent-laden humans deposit customary food in pit, 3) bear hears noisy, scent-laden human(s) depart in customary manner, 3) bear moves to pit to eat customary food — secure though customary, normally-feared, human scent is present — 4) bear fails to realize a human is perched in adjacent tree, the human being silent, motionless and well-camouflaged (a totally unexpected change from the customary behavior exhibited by the humans providing bait) and 5) human shoots unsuspecting bear through heart.

Time of Day to Provide Baits

Upon recognizing early the damage that might be done by disturbing bears feeding at our bait sites, we initially made it rule to never bait before 10AM or after 4PM. Once hunting began — using the two-man, baiting-hunting system (see complete instructions in Chapter 6) — we made a point of baiting between 2:30 and 3:30PM at sites to be hunted, one man silently taking to his tree stand as the other noisily returned to camp.

In time we took note of a predictable difference in the way bears of various ages responded to baiting. At a freshly baited site being regularly visited by multiple bears, the most apt to appear first are one or two of the youngest, independent (not with maternal sows) bears in the area. When weather conditions are favorable, yearlings or 2-1/2-year-olds may rush to a freshly-baited pit within 15-30 minutes after noisy humans have departed. More commonly, they arrive 2-3 hours before sunset. As the sun moves lower in the sky, progressively larger bears show up, younger bears quickly moving away with or without being threatened. The largest bear will likely appear last, either shortly before sunset or after dark.

Discounting younger bears made wary early by harrowing experiences wrought by humans at bait sites, the characteristic timing of their visits — an index of the relative caution of bears of various ages — effectively divided black bears into two distinct groups: 1) bears easy to bait during legal hours, usually small-to-medium in size (up to around 250 pounds) and 2) bears difficult to bait during legal hours, usually large-to-very-large in size (300-500+ pounds).

While this division of black bears held firm at our bait/stand sites, we were occasionally puzzled by long-range sightings of large-to-very-large bears during daylight hours, sometimes even midday. I began to wonder if the timing of bear visits was somehow related to the timing of our baiting. Older bears being more cautious, perhaps they were simply waiting longer before visiting a freshly-baited pit. I decided to try limiting baiting to 10AM - 1PM. It worked, though not at first and not for the reason I expected.

Frustrated by the continuing, mysterious absence of larger bears at bait sites that were visited regularly by larger bears during the two weeks before the hunting season opened, I decided one day to try a different approach. I tiptoed to my stand earlier than usual — six hours before sunset. One-half-hour before sunset, the largest black bear I've ever seen up close in the wilds came to my bait. Before moving near, however, this bear circled through dense timber, remaining out-of-range, until it reached on my trail about 75 yards west of my stand. With great deliberation, it sniffed my trail repeatedly. At length, it turned and followed my trail to the bait pit.

The Rule of Six

All at once I was struck with the realization that this canny bear would not approach my bait site without first assessing the freshness of my human trail scent at a safe distance — safe from a potential human ambush and far enough from the strong odors billowing from the bait pit to be able to make an accurate assessment of the freshness my trail scent possible. All at once I also understood why certain medium-to-large bears in the past, seen moving out-of-range in the vicinity of various bait/stand sites, did not subsequently appear beneath our tree stands — *our human trail scents were too fresh.*

Based on previous and subsequent observations, it became apparent black bears with greater human experience consider certain levels of freshness of human trail scent to be "safe" or "unsafe"— somewhere between five and six hours hours old being the cut-off point for large-to-very-large black bears. Younger bears, it seems, consider fresher human trail scents to be "safe."

From this startling realization was born *The Trophy-Bear Hunter's Rule of Six — when hunting trophy-class black bears, the hunter should not approach a stand/bait site for any purpose, including baiting, less than six hours before sunset.* This rule works. It works in spades.

However, it also imposes some difficult standards. For one, six straight hours of sitting motionless in a tree stand is a physically punishing ordeal. Six straight hours takes planning, preparation, practice, physical and mental stamina and attention to easily-overlooked details like avoiding distress in one's digestive tract and urinary bladder. Six grueling hours at a shot is a ridiculously small price to pay, nonetheless. Most hunters wait a lifetime for a chance at a decent bear, and for many, it never happens.

This rule also sharply delineates when it is best (safe) to haul baits to bait sites while hunting — from 10AM until six hours before sunset (10AM to 1PM in Minnesota during the early part of the bear hunting season).

When baiting before the hunting opener, 10AM to 3PM is acceptable (safe).

Bait Amounts and Frequency of Baiting

Questions concerning the amount of bait that should be used and how frequently it should be provided are subject to a host of variables. Practical answers cannot be arrived at without first finding answers to at least five additional questions: 1) how much bait can the hunter transport to a pit, 2) which is better — daily or less frequent baiting, 3) how many and how large are the bears utilizing baits provided, 4) how long will bears

"Hey guys, take a look at this."

"It's a bear scratch tree.
Look at all the claw marks."

"Looks like a bear trail — wide and flattened."

"It's a bear trail, all right. Here's a big track."

"A bear sure did a job on this tree — probably after honey."

"Sure... here's a ripped-up wasp nest."

"There ought to be a bear or two around here."

"Fresh doughnut-shaped droppings — that settles it. Let's set up a stand."

"How is this for silhouette-hiding cover?"

"This is a perfect spot for a bait pit."

"Timber! Someone come over here and mark off six-foot lengths."

"Only four-hundred and fifty pounds more bait to haul, guys."

"One-hundred and fifty pounds of bait ought to hold 'em awhile."

"There, that does it. If this doesn't attract bears soon, nothing will."

"Look at that! They cleaned us out."

"Wow...check the size of this track! This bear will easily go four-hundred pounds or more!"

"Here's a good way to toughen up the draggin' crew."

"Keepin' our bait and food on this platform ought to keep those black critters out of our tent tonight."

"Here, I'll give you a hand."

"How do I look?"

"Don't worry, buck — I'm huntin' bears this time."

"That big one won't be so cautious when he gets a whiff of this honey."

"I'll bet a bear is bedded right now over in those cedars."

"Keep your mouth shut, squirrel."

"Oh-oh...here comes a bear!"

"A perfect heart shot from five yards with a bow — how about that?"

"It just doesn't get any better!"

remain in the vicinity of a bait site after baits are exhausted and 5) how does frequency of baiting affect hunting success on opening day?

My son, Dave, can haul 150 pounds of bait on a plastic sled over 1/2-mile of cleared trail with only one stop for a breather. Having a bad ankle, 75 pounds is my limit. When I'm baiting, therefore (insisting on hauling in at least 150 pounds of bait to each pit), it's a two-man, two-sled (two-cans-of-pop) operation. Most hunters should easily handle 75 pounds strapped in a sled..

The more often a hunter travels to a bait pit, the greater becomes the risk of spooking a bear there. Whereas stumbling into a younger bear at a pit may not be serious, the bear returning a day or two later, such a mishap may easily spell doom when an older bear is involved. The older bear may not return at all, it may return during nighttime hours only, or it may return during daylight hours again, but only after a considerable time has elapsed, perhaps 2-3 weeks. For this reason, I prefer to haul in larger amounts of bait less often — 150 pounds every 4-7 days. The frequency within this time frame depends on how many and/or how large the bears are that are consuming bait at a pit, and time remaining before opening day.

A 400-500 pound black bear will consume 40-50 pounds of bait daily; a 100-125 pound yearling, 15-20 pounds daily. Because few, if any, black bears will dare to feed at a bait pit claimed by a 400-500 bear, 150 pounds of bait will usually hold such a bear 4-6 days, the bear feeding heavily 3-4 days; then, perhaps, gnawing on bones during normal feeding cycles over another 1-2 days. Most larger bears will take to regular forage routes within 24 hours after bait is exhausted. With a bear that has hind paw prints measuring 8-1/2 or more inches in length, it is best to bait every 4-5 days.

Lots of bait less often is "big bear" medicine.

Where multiple bears are visiting a pit, hind tracks will usually measure 7–1/2 inches or less in length (100-250 pound bears). In most cases, no more than 3-5 bears will regularly visit a bait pit. Once, we had eight feeding regularly at one pit, two being twin cubs with a dour sow about 250 pounds in size. Three medium-sized bears will not usually empty a pit in less than 4-5 days, and generally they'll continue checking the pit daily up to a week after the bait is exhausted. For 3-5 small-to-medium-sized bears, once-a-week baiting (150 pounds per baiting) is usually adequate.

Baiting becomes legal in Minnesota two weeks before the opener. We generally wait a week after our initial baiting to bait again, reasoning, even if a large bear has hit a pit early during the first week, it will surely return again sometime during the second week. Our most crucial baiting occurs 3-4 days before the opener. This baiting insures there will be bears — all classes — visiting our baits during the first two days of hunting

As a rule, we bait again at noon on opening day. That is usually enough, but just in case, we like to keep 200-300 pounds of bait in reserve while hunting, so we can add bait when and where needed. There's nothing worse than being caught short on bait when hunting.

Chapter 5

Preparing to Hunt Black Bears

Effective Weaponry

Points to Consider

1. When firing at a black bear, the average bow or firearm hunter is four times *less* accurate, or worse, than when firing at a stationary target at a practice range.

2. At a bait/stand site, the hunter will rarely have more than one shooting opportunity at a black bear — at the shot, even a heart-shot bear will bolt from sight within the blink of an eye.

3. The heart/lung region of the largest black bear is smaller in size than that of an adult white-tailed buck and surrounded by heavier muscle and bone.

4. The largest heart-shot black bear will succumb within 15-20 seconds. A large lung-shot black bear (no heart involvement) can travel up to 200 yards after the shot. A bear hit in any other area — other than the spine or brain — may live several days, perhaps traveling 20 miles or more (if pushed by high-profile hunters) through the most impregnable swamps.

5. The upper two-thirds of a black bear's body is covered with heavy muscle, soft fat and thick fur, all of which can effectively seal a wound. A single, high body wound (no matter how fatal) will not produce much in the way of blood sign, making tracking very difficult, if not impossible. A low exit wound, heart and/or lung tissue damaged, will bleed profusely, making tracking very easy. Many black bears are wasted — they die and are not recovered in time to save the carcass and hide, if at all — when hit by shots that are not quickly fatal and/or by by shots that do not produce an easy-to-follow blood trail.

6. The heavy scapula (wide shoulder bone), vertebrae (spine) or skull of any black bear will abruptly halt the penetration of any arrow, preventing damage to vital underlying tissues. The heavy scapula or spine of a large bear may greatly limit the penetration (and damage to vital tissues) of a mushrooming bullet.

7. A shot that merely breaks a shoulder bone will do little in the way of slowing down a black bear — a black bear can travel almost as fast and as far on three legs as on four.

8. The largest, unalarmed black bear is easier to kill (it will die more quickly) that an adult white-tailed deer, using the same weaponry. A wounded black bear — its adrenalin surging — is much more difficult to kill than an unsuspecting, unwounded bear.

9. The potential for being injured by a black bear is greatest when trailing a live, wounded black bear.

10. If the average bear hunter's marksmanship is equal to the average whitetail hunter's marksmanship, the number of crippled and lost black bears is likely equal to the number of registered bear kills — *an enormous threat to the future of black bears and black bear hunting.*

Exit Wound Capability

Considering the above, the single most important prerequisite of any bullet, slug or arrow intended for use on a black bear is, it must be capable of penetrating completely through a bear's chest — it must make a low exit wound (the probable result when a shot is fired from an elevated stand). Many hunters may insist that anything legal, anything capable of killing a white-tailed deer or anything capable of penetrating deeply enough to damage a bear's lungs or heart is good enough. "Good enough," however, does not square with the following facts: 1) average hunters are not skilled marksmen and 2) average hunters are not skilled at recovering wounded game. Lacking tracking snow or an obvious blood trail the average hunter's odds for recovering a wounded bear that travels more than 200 yards are slim at best.

Firepower, a head or neck shot or a string tracker (archery) are not good alternatives to a low exit wound.

The Myth of Firepower

To some, firepower means "a potent cartridge — one that is fast and/or heavy and deadly." Whereas some may consider a black bear dangerous enough to warrant using a .375 Weatherby Magnum, even when shot through the lungs (heart untouched) with this potent cartridge, nine of ten medium-to-large black bears will not drop in their tracks as might be expected. Within a few sudden leaps, they'll be plunging 30 mph through the darnedest cover imaginable and they may not go down until they have covered 150-200 yards.

Most hunters today define firepower as the ability to fire several shots very rapidly, as when using a semi-automatic rifle. Most hunters who use automatics (I too used one many years ago) realize they might not hit what they aim at with the first shot, so they covet the idea of a quick second shot. Realizing they may not hit anything with the second shot either, they are comforted by the knowledge they can quickly fire a third shot if needed...and so on. Some hunters using semi-automatics simply point and empty their rifles as quickly as possible, using a sort of a shotgun approach — hoping at least one shot will hit the target. Shooting in this manner at a rifle range, such a hunter would be lucky to put one bullet into a 10-inch circle at 100 yards. With a live bear to shoot at, the bear will likely live to a ripe, old age.

It matters little whether you are partial to a semi-automatic, pump, lever action or bolt action rifle. When hunting black bears over bait, all you're likely to get is one shot. A five-shot magazine that can be quickly emptied cannot make you a safer or more successful bear hunter.

Risky Head and Neck Shots

Sad is the hunter who attempts a brain shot. A black bear's brain is smaller than its heart, making the brain a difficult target. Hit anywhere else in the head — the brain undamaged — the hunter is in for a long and tough trailing assignment, perhaps harrowing as well.

Actually hitting the brain can be almost as great a disaster. When a modern big game cartridge penetrates a bear's brain cavity at short range, it's skull will virtually explode. The hunter will have a bear hide, but no head. Black bears make much-revered trophies. It's difficult to imagine anyone shooting a black bear without having its head and hide made into a handsome and impressive wall mount or rug. A head shot will destroy that opportunity (perhaps a once-in-a-lifetime opportunity). Don't shoot a bear in the head unless you are gravely threatened and then unless you have no other quick-kill target to shoot at.

A medium-to-large bear's neck is an extremely "iffy" target. Large bears have very thick necks. The vital tissues inside — the spinal cord and large blood vessels — occupy a curved space not much more than two inches wide, top-to-bottom. Not only is this vital tissue a very small target, but it is extremely difficult to determine where it is situated within a bear's enormous neck. If you only hit muscle, you are going to have a very difficult time attempting to properly finish your bear.

A bowhunter I talked to last fall shot a yearling in the neck without a quickly fatal effect. With very little blood sign, he nonetheless managed to stay on the bear's trail over a period of three days. I have to give this hunter enormous credit. He did a masterful job of recovering his bear. The average hunter could not have done it.

String Trackers

If string trackers did exactly what they are supposed to do, every time, and without significantly reducing arrow velocity and penetration, I'd encourage (demand) every bowhunter to use one for black bear hunting. The trouble is, they don't always work and they greatly reduce arrow velocity. You can personally find out how much they reduce arrow speed by comparing arrow speeds on a chronograph at an archery range. I know several hunters who have had opportunities at trophy bucks ruined by strings that refused to flow smoothly at the shot, and I've heard plenty of sad tales about strings that snarled in brush and broke off. Worst of all, an arrow slowed by a string tracker is very unlikely to penetrate through a bear's chest. I personally want none of these problems when hunting bears with a bow.

Last fall, I put an arrow through the chest of a 422-pound black bear. Driving a 2117 arrow with a 150 grain Muzzy broadhead from my 60-pound Onieda Eagle 500 at a range of five yards, the broadhead exited only an inch or so beneath the bear's right foreleg after passing through the upper portion of the bear's heart. With that, the bear plunged 165 yards through an alder swamp before dropping dead. The entry wound did not bleed. The exit wound bled profusely. I think I could have felt my way to the bear with my eyes closed. Without that exit wound, it not only would have been tough to find this bear, the bear would probably have spoiled — meat and hide — before I could have found and transported it from the woods to a locker plant.

One could argue that I would not have needed that exit wound if I was using a string tracker. Feeling certain I was at last going to shoot a trophy-class bruin, however, I simply could not bear the thought of a string failing to uncoil smoothly or the thought of standing in a swamp afterwards, starring forlornly at a tangle of broken string. No, rather than add a potential problem or two, I went with what I absolutely knew I'd get without a tracker — maximum arrow penetration and a low, heavily-bleeding exit wound. Everything worked perfectly. When hunting black bears, I'll take a reliable exit wound blood trail every time over a string.

Recommended Weaponry

Although there is nothing wrong with using magnum bullets on black bears, long-range, flat-shooting bullets will not provide any particular advantage when shooting bears at at a range of 10-20 yards. All that really matters is, the bullet must pass through the heart/lung region and make an exit wound. As long as heavier-grained bullets are used, I can't think of a single, modern day, 30mm cartridge that will fail to do that. Although I'd feel more at ease with a 30-06 or .308 in my lap, even a 30-30 will do the job. Deadly on black bears are 150 grain .270s and 175 grain 7mm Remington Magnums. A 175 grain 7mm Remington Magnum will zip right through a bear's chest without any problem. The lighter 150 grain bullet, however, is unlikely to make an exit wound. I wouldn't use smaller calibers like a .243 or 6mm Remington. Though these calibers will certainly kill black bears, they are very unlikely to make it it all the way through a bear's chest. I don't think I'd care to use a .44 Magnum either, but the .444 Marlin should have what it takes. At 20 yards or less, a 12-gauge slug from a shotgun with accurate sights can be devastating bear medicine.

Open sights or a 1X scope are recommended. With more than 2X, within 20 yards it can be very difficult to determine which part of a bear one is aiming at (all you'll see is black hair).

Though a lot of bowhunters will shriek when I say this, I really believe you're under-gunned for black bears when using anything less than a standard arrow with a 150 grain broadhead and a 60-pound bow. You need maximum foot-pounds energy to zip an arrow through a 200-pound bear with lesser equipment, but when a 400-500 pounder shows up, even with the above equipment, you're just barely adequate. If you can manage a heavier bow, do it. I'm planning to move up to 70 pounds myself.

A standard arrow, 150-grain broadhead and a 60-70 pound bow are as deadly out to 20 yards as a 7mm. Remington Magnum.

Developing "Perfect Bear Shot" Marksmanship

No matter how experienced the hunter, preparing to shoot at a black bear at short range is like lining up on a 20-foot putt on the final green to win the Masters Golf Tournament at Augusta. The pressure might make even a three-foot putt impossible (ask Hubert Green). Most hunters — even those with 50 years of experience — feel the same sort of pressure when aiming at a large white-tailed buck. When the quarry is a large black bear — a potentially dangerous beast with devastating power and evil-looking fangs and claws — the pressure and its effects far outclass mere "buck fever."

Pressure of this sort is highly destructive to the process of making an accurate shot, whether at Augusta National Golf Course or at a bait/stand site. Adrenalin and blood sugar are the culprits — human chemicals that surge into the bloodstream during moments of great excitement or peril. They prepare the body for super-human efforts during fight or flight. For ancient man, adrenalin and blood sugar probably made it possible to overtake and kill wild animals with simple, hand-held weapons such as spears or clubs. These normal body chemicals, unfortunately, work against man's ability to make the finite physical adjustments necessary to make controlled, accurate shots with gun or bow. They not only trigger a strong blood flow (a strong heart beat) and a trembling of the limbs, but they not uncommonly cause a sudden loss in sensory perception and willful thought. Panic, whether caused by a fear of danger or a fear of blundering, contributes to the problem, bizarre behavior not uncommonly the outcome. Many hunters will suddenly become unable to perceive the sights on their weapons. Some will suddenly find it impossible to draw their bows. Some will react by by shooting wildly and rapidly, sometimes straight up into the air, and some will eject unfired cartridges until their rifles until empty, totally unaware of their actions. Faced by a black bear, some hunters have thrown their weapons to the ground and fled with with all possible speed. Some have fallen from their stands. However affected, almost all hunters become clumsy in the the presence of a bear, unable to shoot accurately and in danger of being identified as a result of uncontrolled motions and inadvertent sounds.

Considering all this, there should be little wonder why hunters have always been so doggone proud of themselves when they actually succeed in killing a bear.

Can anything be done to control these very human responses? Is an accurate, one-shot bear kill possible? Sure. Do it as follows:

Develop a Shooting Groove

A shooting groove is a series of *instinctive* actions that lead to reliable, accurate shots. Especially when preparing to shoot at a bear, the hunter must lean heavily on well-established — instinctive — actions. This is no time to wonder whether you are doing things right. If you must wonder about such things at this point, you won't do things right because you won't be capable of thinking properly. Well before you begin hunting, your mind and body must be programed to go through the motions of aiming and firing accurately without a great deal of conscious thought — everything must become instinctive.

No human is born with the instincts necessary for shooting a bow or firearm accurately under pressure. Every step in must be learned; then repeated over and over again until the entire process finally becomes instinctive. It takes good instruction initially; then practice, practice and more practice. It is as ludicrous to believe a bear hunter can become an expert bear shot (develop that groove) after only one hour of practice as it is to believe a golfer or a bowler can become a pro after only one hour of practice. Yet the majority of those who hunt bear or deer today do it with no more practice than that. It takes months of regular shooting to develop a groove. Being the klutz I am, it took me two years — shooting almost daily during spring, summer and fall — to develop a groove and become accurate enough to trust myself to take on a bear with a bow.

Foolish is the hunter who hunts black bears without first becoming absolutely confident of personal shooting ability. That's where most of the self-imposed pressure comes from, and all the self-destructive physical responses that follow — lacking confidence.

The process of developing reliable shooting instincts need not be confined to the practice range. Much can be accomplished at home, without cost. By repeatedly raising your rifle (unloaded) or bow (coming to a full draw) and and fixing your sights on random targets in the privacy of your basement or garage — going through each step exactly as if in the field, but not firing — over a period of time a most important part of your shooting groove will become well ingrained. Moreover, the muscles involved in shooting will become stronger and steadier. Your actions will become smoother and more direct. The benefits of such practice — dry firing — will become very evident when actually firing at a shooting range; also when drawing a bead on a bear.

Become an Expert Marksman

How many times have you heard the following?

BAM-BAM-BAM-BAM-BAM! Not bad — five of ten shots in a ten-inch circle. Shooting like that, I certainly ought to be able to hit a deer. These automatics never pattern well, but I'll tell you, this is a real meat gun. Something must be wrong with my scope. I don't understand it — I had'im dead to rights. What are you shooting from a bench rest for? You can't take a bench rest with you in the woods. After a dozen arrows or so, I usually start putting 'em right in there.

Plenty of hunters guilty of such acts and words hunt black bears. Though they might be good talkers, convincing others they are deadly shots (etc.), with live bears before them, it is unlikely any of this ilk is capable of shooting a bear in the lungs, much less the heart.

Because it is unnecessary to shoot at a bear from a distance of more than 10-20 yards, it probably doesn't seem logical that it would take extraordinary skill to be an expert bear shot. How accurate do you have to be? **Since almost all hunters will be at least four-times *less* accurate when shooting at a live bear, and since a bear's heart measures about 3 X 5 inches in size, the hunter must be capable of hitting a 1-inch circle with *every shot* — using firearm or bow — at a range of 10-20 yards during practice. Not four out of five — *every shot*. Especially *every first shot*.**

Even at such a short range, 1-inch accuracy demands all of the tricks needed to achieve the same accuracy at longer ranges. Sights or scopes must be precisely aligned, bows must be perfectly tuned and the marksman usually must make use of various shooting aids. As the hunting season draws near, that typically errant first shot must become as reliable as the last. When a bear comes in, warm-up shots are out of question.

Whatever you do, don't settle for lesser accuracy. If you're having trouble, get some professional advice. Ask a rifle or archery rangemaster to watch what you're doing. You may be flinching, holding your rifle or bow wrong or maybe something is wrong with your equipment. The addition of a sling, recoil pad, new scope, improved arrow rest, bow stabilizer, mechanical release or string peep might make all the difference in the world. If you find you cannot achieve the necessary accuracy beyond 10 or 15 yards, then make certain your bait pits are located no more than 10 or 15 yards from your stands.

There is no way you are going to get by with cheating on accuracy. You won't be able to fool your own mind. Unless you can honestly tell yourself, "No doubt about it, I can shoot this bear in the heart," when the time comes — *I guarantee it* **— you will suffer the worst case of "buck fever" you've ever known.**

Count on being somewhat un-

Sitting, rifle braced against tree, the hunter will be four-times more accurate than when shooting offhand.

nerved when the comes time to to shoot at a bear. You can bet your pickup your arms and legs will be trembling. That's normal — everyone does it, some more than others. Those who claim otherwise, flat-out lie. There is no rule that states you must shoot off-hand under these circumstances. There is nothing "sporting" about shooting off-hand while your body is shaking. This is not a game in which you get points for a near-miss. If you wound a bear, it is unlikely it will survive to be shot at another day. Like all bear hunters who routinely make one-shot, quick kills, use every trick necessary to steady your aim.

When using a rifle, like when using a bench rest at the practice range, shoot from a sitting position. This will cancel the effect of of your trembling knees. Then use a rest to cancel the effect of trembling arms. Brace the forearm of your rifle against the trunk of a tree, or plant your left elbow (if right handed) against something solid like your left thigh or a part of your stand. Practice doing this until you can be sure it will all be automatic when a bear shows up.

Similarly, when using a bow, shoot from a sitting position. Once you get the hang of it, not only will you be thankful you won't have to stand up while a big bruin nibbles corn beneath your stand, but you'll happily discover you can actually shoot more accurately from a sitting position. Begin shooting exclusively from a sitting position well before the hunting season begins. Find your best angle to the target — the one that gives you the best accuracy without strain and without interference from your stand. Make sure your stands are positioned to give you every advantage.

If you think your arms may shake enough to ruin your aim while using a bow, there's nothing wrong with lashing or nailing a vertical pole to the left of your stand platform against which you can brace your extended left arm while taking aim. When bear hunting over bait, you can make use of such a rest with remarkable precision. If you plan to use a rest, however, be sure to practice with one at home, leaving nothing to chance.

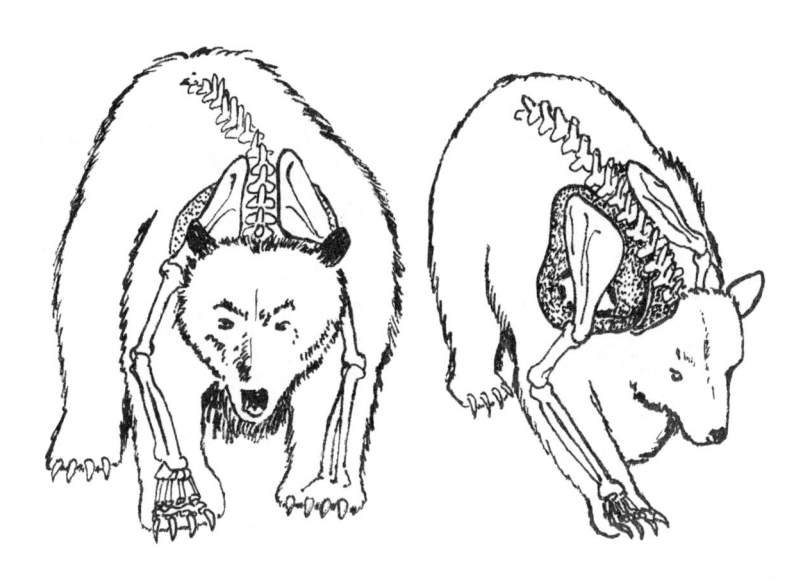

From a stand, it is virtually impossible to hit a bear's heart while it is facing the hunter.

Quartering toward the hunter, a bears heart is well-protected by heavy shoulder bones.

Recognize Effective Heart Shot Angles

First-shot, one-inch accuracy at two-dimensional targets is only the beginning. The hunter must also learn to visualize the exact position of a bear's heart buried deep within a three-dimensional figure made up of hair, muscle and bone. Spatial visualization of the positions of the heart, spine, scapula and leg bones is especially critical to bowhunting.

Quartering away, the path to a bear's heart is clear of all intervening bones—1 of 2 acceptable bow shots.

Standing broadside, near foreleg vertical, a bear's heart is guarded by heavy shoulder bones.

Concentrate on Making the Shot

Generally, it takes a great deal of patience to wait for an open, proper shot angle when hunting black bears over bait. As a rule, from the moment a bear is sighted moving toward a bait pit, 5-15 nerve-racking minutes will pass before a quick-kill shot is possible. Unfortunately, humans are not noted for having that much patience, more especially when plagued by the electrifying excitement typical of a short-range encounter with a bear. Once a bear is spotted, the average hunter's first inclination

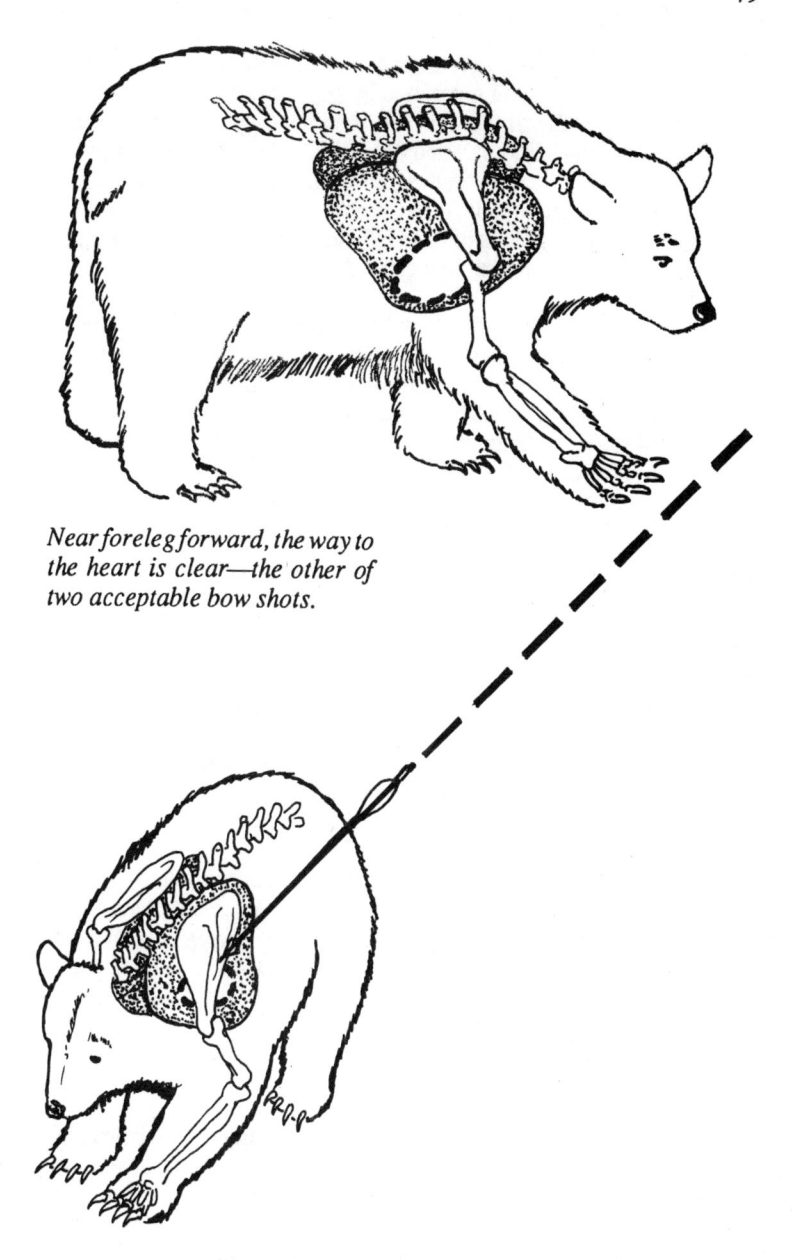

Near foreleg forward, the way to the heart is clear—the other of two acceptable bow shots.

When firing at a bear situated within 20 yards from a stand height significantly greater than 12 feet, heavy shoulder bones line up over the bear's heart.

is to shoot as quickly as possible. For some, it's simply a matter of normal thought processes being derailed by super-excitement and/or panic. Some hunters pull the trigger quickly knowing they will become basket cases in short order. Football and basketball coaches play on this well-known human weakness by calling time-outs just before field goals or penalty shots are attempted, often with heartbreaking success. Most often, quick-shooting leads to unsatisfactory results — the approaching bear is missed (unnoticed branches deflecting the shot) or merely wounded.

The thing to remember is, black bears lured by baits will likely stick around for some time, 15-60 minutes or more, barring detection of the hunter. There is absolutely no reason to hurry the shot from the bear's standpoint. Success in black bear hunting over bait, then, is not so much a matter of a hunter's mastery over a bear, but more a matter of a hunter's mastery over his or her own skyrocketing emotions.

How do you control your emotions in this situation? There's only one way to do it that I know of — like pro golfers, shut all distractions from your mind. Concentrate wholly on the mechanics of making an accurate shot.

In this case, the distraction is the bear. As quickly as you can, erase from your mind's eye the bear. Concentrate only on what you must do to get ready for the shot. As you raise your weapon — ever so slowly — watch carefully your hands and your weapon, making sure no part touches anything. At this point, the slightest unnatural sound can be ruinous. Continue in this manner until you are ready to ease your index finger to the trigger of your rifle, or until you have come to a full draw. Now, return your attention to the bear. Not the whole bear — only it's quick-kill target area — that window surrounded by bones through which you will shoot to hit the bear's underlying heart. Concentrate on that spot, waiting if you must for a favorable shot angle. When it looks right, lock your sight or scope reticle on the correct spot in that furry window. Begin your squeeze, visualizing the bear's heart beneath. Quite suddenly, a heart-shot bear will streak from your bait pit clearing.

That's how you do it.

Hunting Gear

The following is a list of hunting gear I personally take to bear camp. I feel each item is essential. Each contributes something to bear hunting, or might, depending on circumstances. This list is not intended to be "the standard" for every black bear hunter. Hunting, whatever the quarry, is a highly individualized sport. This is a *good* list, however, one that has yet to fail me. Whatever happens, I'm confident it's covered. Underlined items are those I carry to my stands when hunting.

1. **Bow**, case, **quiver, hunting arrows**, practice arrows, **hunting broadheads**, practice broadheads, field target, spare string, bow stringer, bow tools, **arm guard, mechanical release, 20-foot cord** and/or **rifle with sling and scope**, case, cleaning kit, **cartridges**, paper targets and tacks.

The bow, arrows and broadheads I personally use were identified above. All parts of my bow, including rest, plunger, sight assembly and quiver are covered with non-glare camouflage paints. Though my rubber-lined, detachable (for auto transport) quiver will hold six arrows, I never carry more than four. I've never had to use more than one arrow on a bear.

Though my single-pin sight — good for dead-on aiming out to 30 yards — arrow rest, plunger and nocking bead rarely need adjusting, I nonetheless take practice equipment — extra arrows tipped with practice broadheads and a nine-spot field target (shooting at one spot is hard on arrows) to camp so I can practice daily to keep my first-shot accuracy sharp.

My mechanical release is the type that attaches to my right wrist with a Velcro strap. I'm partial to this release because rather than weaker (shakier) finger muscles, my larger and stronger (steadier) arm and shoulder muscles are in sole command when drawing my bow. This not only enhances accuracy (for me), but if I am obliged to hold a full draw for a lengthy period, these larger muscles can endure the strain much longer than my fingers could.

Because you never know when a bow string will begin fraying, I always keep an extra on hand, ready-to-go. Ready-to-go means I've had the new string on my bow, I've added silencers, a nocking bead and string peep sight, and I've shot with it, making all necessary adjustments to assure quick accuracy when the time comes to put it into service. Even with all this pre-use, time-saving preparation, of course, I'll check a newly-mounted string thoroughly again before hunting with it.

The 20-foot cord — dyed brown — is used to safely (safe for my weapon and me) raise and lower my bow or unloaded rifle at my stand platform. It is knotted about every 12 inches to prevent slipping.

The rifle I have long used for black bear hunting is a Model 77 Ruger bolt action chambered for 7mm Remington Magnum, a sling added and topped with a 2-7X Vari-Power Leopold scope. For bears at baits, I set the scope on 2-power (widest field). I use 175-grain Remington Core-Lock cartridges (three punched down in the magazine though I've never had to use more than one bullet on a bear).

The targets and tacks always accompany my rifle to camp. Their only purpose is to be handy for making finite adjustments (far from my hunting area) in the event my scope has been roughly jarred or found to be out of alignment. In the 23 years I have owned this rifle, I've only found it necessary to readjust my scope while hunting once (a horse rolled on it).

2. Field dressing knife, pocket knife, an oiled sharpening stone, two feet of heavy string, a five-foot length of paper toweling, three one-gallon-sized plastic bags and ties and a partial roll of toilet paper

My field dressing/skinning knife has a wide, curved, 2-1/2 inch blade. It is ideal for many purposes, especially ideal when reaching forward into the tight quarters of a bear's chest to severe the windpipe, esophagus and large blood vessels when field dressing a bear. Though it holds an edge longer than any knife I have ever used, I have long made it a practice to carry a sharpening stone to my stand to make sure I will never be without a sharp knife. The stone is sealed in a plastic bag (to prevent the escape of the odor of oil).

The heavy string is needed to tie-off a bear's urethra and rectum during field dressing. The paper toweling is intended for wiping blood from hands after field dressing is complete. In an emergency, it also makes a good fire starter. One of the plastic bags is intended to be used as a container for a bear's heart — a favorite Nordberg camp delicacy following a bear kill. The toilet paper — unscented — is intended to be used to mark a shot bear's trail, should the bear prove to be difficult to find (more on recovering a wounded bear later).

The other two plastic bags are my stand potty. One is placed inside the other and each is sealed separately after the inner bag is used. I've used plastic bags for this purpose more than twenty years without a mishap. When leaving a stand, a used potty bag is taken back to camp and dumped in the latrine. A potty bag is an important aid to bear hunting success. When bear hunting — especially when hunting a big bear — it is not only ruinous to urinate anywhere within 200 yards of a bait/stand site, but it can be equally ruinous to leave a stand for this purpose between 1PM and nightfall.

3. Compass, map, matches (in a waterproof container), steel tape and digital watch

These tools are constant companions whether hunting bears or deer, the first three of obvious importance in off-trail wilderness navigation and survival. The steel tape is kept handy to measure and identify bears by the lengths of their hind paw prints. Because bears can hear a ticking watch when within 20 yards, I use a silent digital. I prefer a cheap, colored, plastic watch, rather than one with a metal case because it will not be as readily seen by a bear. My watch is an important adjunct to my bear hunting. It enhances my patience, tells me when to bait, when to head to my stand, when to be especially attentive and when legal shooting hours are over.

4. Small packsack, headnet, insect lotion, safety strap, binoculars, flashlight (6-volt and D-battery), sunglasses and fox urine with applicator

Obviously, I could not carry all the paraphernalia I need for bear hunting in my pockets. In fact, I prefer to keep my pockets empty to eliminate the possibility of making unexpected jingles (unnatural sounds) while a bear is beneath my stand. Thus I routinely carry a small, waterproof, camouflage packsack (standpack), hanging it within easy reach on a branch or tree step as soon as I climb to my stand platform.

"Standard" in my pack is a headnet, used not only to ward off insects, but to camouflage my eyeglasses or sunglasses when the sun is shining directly on my face.

Also "standard" is my safety strap.

A flashlight — I usually carry a 2-D-battery type — is also an essential. As a black bear hunter, not only will you regularly leave your stand in darkness, but upon shooting a bear, you'll end up doing all sorts of work in the dark. Extra batteries and bulbs should always be kept on hand in camp.

When hunting, I routinely apply fox urine to my boots before heading to a bait/stand site and again before climbing to the ground to leave a stand (see Chapter 5, "Applying Fox Urine")

5. Facial camo, mirror, camo cleaner, wash basin, unscented soap, washcloth, towel and a five-gallon jug of water.

All of these items are for applying and removing facial camouflage.

6. Plastic sled, tie-ropes, heavy-duty plastic yard bags and ties

The plastic sled and assorted short lengths of ropes (used to tie bait containers securely in the sled) are basic tools of the bear baiter/hunter. So are lots of large, heavy-duty yard bags, used to protect and seal (eliminating bear-attracting odors) baits and human foods in camp.

7. A 30-foot, 1/2-inch Manila rope, 100 feet of 1/4-inch nylon rope, a 9' X 12' reinforced heavy-duty plastic tarp, a hand-operated 1000-pound winch and about eight screw-in tree steps

This is "bear handling equipment" – explained in Chapter 6 (see "Transporting a Bear Carcass to Camp").

8. Shovel, axe, bow saw, rake, chainsaw, chainsaw gas, chainsaw oil, bar oil, leather gloves and tools

Folding, screw-in steps used to climb to stands.

This equipment will be frequently used during a bear hunt — in camp, at bait/stand sites and when transporting a bear carcass to camp.

9. Gas lantern, extra mantels, lantern gas and funnel

If you find it necessary to trail a shot bear in the dark, there is nothing like the light of a 2-mantel Coleman lantern for making bear blood easy to spot. It'll appear almost fluorescent. I also consider a gas lantern to be an absolute necessity for field dressing a black bear in the dark — invariably the case. Of all the bears my sons, son-in-law and I have shot, only two were field dressed during daylight hours. Once I've ascertained my bear is down and dead, I will not hesitate to hike a mile or more to get my ancient gas lantern. Following field dressing, a gas lantern is also handy for lighting the trail at the head of a struggling drag crew. With a wide field of illumination, there'll be far less stumbling, eye-gouging, falling and swearing, there'll be fewer windfalls to haul the bear carcass over and the bear hide will suffer far less wear and tear.

10. First-aid kit

Be sure to include plenty of antiseptic, gauze, tape, bandages, bee sting medication and burn ointment. A couple of ace bandages might be a good idea too. Scrapes, cuts, stings, burns and sprains are not uncommon maladies in bear camp.

11. Camera gear, including flash and extra batteries and film

Don't miss the chance to record on film forever your once-in-a-lifetime adventure (also the chance to gain the undeniable evidence that will give you *braggin' rights* the rest of your days). More than likely, you'll need a flash camera.

12. High-top rubber boots, hipboots and sneakers

The high-top rubber boots are for baiting and hunting. The hipboots are a backup, used when necessary to trail a shot bear in a wet swamp (shot bears love wet swamps). It's nice to get out of rubber boots at the end of the day and don a comfortable pair of sneakers.

13. <u>Camo</u> rainsuit

When it rains in the fall, my sons, son-in-law and I call it "bear hunting weather." For some strange reason, it seems to rain a lot in early September when we do most of our bear hunting. As we've learned, bears accustomed to finding food at bait pits are little bothered by rain unless it's heavy. A good camo rainsuit is much more than just something practical to wear when it is raining — it's a vital bear hunting tool.

Unfortunately, even the best rainsuits fall short of being ideal for bear hunting. Most are made of noisy fabric, you perspire inside when exerting yourself (despite claims that you won't), they're cold and clammy after a few hours in a tree stand, their seams begin leaking and sharp branches, tree steps and saw blades inevitably take their toll. Well before a bear hunt begins, it is prudent to check your rainsuit thoroughly, patching holes and re-sealing seams and/or spraying the fabric with water proofing. After such repairs are made, a rainsuit should be aired outside for several days to get rid of strong, unnatural odors.

14. Camo clothing — shirts, pants, belt, cap or hat, T-shirts, handkerchiefs, <u>sweater</u>, <u>jacket</u> and <u>cotton gloves</u>

All exposed clothing must be made with a camo pattern and colors that closely match the tree you sit in at your bait/stand site. It should be soft (quiet) and as free of unnatural odors as possible (and kept that way — sealed in odorless plastic bags). If you're a bowhunter, your cap or hat should not interfere with your string during a full draw. Because you will be constantly handling unnatural things with your gloves, plan to wear a fresh pair daily.

15. Underwear and socks

You may not realize it until your hunting clothes have been sitting in a basket in the laundry room for a week, but a hard-working bear hunter's clothing will quickly become a horrendous source of a heady and unnatural odors. Each day in camp, after washing your skin (head-to-toe) with a scentless soap, you should don a fresh, clean set of underwear and socks.

16. Camp clothing

A common mistake among hunters is to smoke, cook, handle foods and other malodorous items or spend time in local watering spots or restaurants while wearing their hunting clothes. In doing this their clothes become loaded with very effective bear repellants. Upon arriving at camp at the end of the day, this enormous error can be avoided by immediately removing outer hunting clothes, re-sealing them in odorless plastic bags, and then putting on camp clothes. Wear camp clothes when not hunting; hunting clothes when hunting only. Be sure to bring everything you might need for comfort in camp so you won't have to "borrow" any item of hunting clothing.

17. Bait-hauling clothing

Though the clothing you wear while hauling baits will certainly become heady with the odors of baits and perspiration, like hunting clothing, it should be protected from contamination by new and strange odors common to bear camp.

18. Toilet kit, including baking soda, scentless soap, scentless bath towels and scentless washcloths

When hunting bears, do not apply anything to your body or hair that is scented. Rather that toothpaste, use baking soda to brush your teeth. Your towels and washcloths, like your hunting clothing, should have been washed with a scentless soap, hung outside to dry and sealed in scentless plastic bags before taken to camp. These too should be protected from tobacco and cooking odors.

18. Bait

Opening weekend, I take enough bait to fill each pit 1-1/2 times — 225 pounds per pit.

Personal Scent Management

Obviously, many of the items I take to bear camp are intended to aid in the never-ending struggle to fool a black bear's nose. I am in awe of the black bear's ability to detect odors originating from high in trees (and tree stands). Whereas I work hard to condition baited bears to become accustomed to smelling my characteristic odors, I feel it is important to prevent the introduction of new and strange odors at bait/stand sites while hunting. New and strange odors many not intimidate younger bears, but older, wiser bears have proven (to me) over and over again that they are indeed intimidated by new and strange odors, especially if fresh and strong. Though eliminating new and strange odors can be tough to accomplish and though it's even tougher to prove such prevention is absolutely necessary, I am nonetheless convinced success in hunting trophy-class bears is almost wholly dependent on how skillfully the hunter manages scents — going to the stand early to avoid freshness, for example, and avoiding odor contamination of hunting clothing, for another. Whatever the size of the bear, the extra effort required to remain odor-free generally pays off. The relatively scentless hunter will always see greater numbers of unalarmed bears (or deer) at short range than the hunter who reeks (by bear nose standards) of unnatural odors.

Bear Camp

The list of the equipment and foods I traditionally use to provide a comfortable bear camp would serve no useful purpose, I think, the reason being, I'm a devout (all-weather) tent camper, almost alone today in a camping world dominated by motorhomes, motorcoaches, tent trailers and pickup campers. As long as a hunting camp provides the basics — good sleep, good food and protection from wet, cold and insects — who am I to judge whether one man's "ideal camp" is superior to another's? When camping while hunting black bears, however, there are a few important precautions to keep in mind, . What you do in camp and where you camp can not only affect hunting success, but it can have everything to do with how much you'll enjoy camping while hunting black bears. Here's some important DON'Ts:

Don't give bears a reason to break into your tent, trailer or vehicle. Though you may camp at a long familiar site — the spot where you camp when hunting deer, for example — at no time will you be more likely to be visited by one or more bears. There are two good reasons for this. For one, bears will be moving more freely. Unlike during a typical deer hunting season, your camp will probably be the only camp within miles, meaning bears will be far less intimidated by humans.

Secondly, the bears you've been baiting know you are the one providing food. By the time you begin to set up your camp, these bears will recognize the sounds of your vehicle and even your voice. To them, these sounds have an exciting meaning — *great food.* Being their "good buddy,"— not at all a threat (up to this point) — some of your baited bears may not wait long to pay you a visit, wondering, perhaps, if you are now also providing food where you are camping. If a baited bear smells familiar odors emanating from a tent, trailer or vehicle, you can bet it will reason something like this: *"Hmmm...that human is providing food here too. In those other places (bait/stand sites), this human hides my food under under logs. Here, it's different, but a big, log-rippin' brute like me will have no trouble gettin' to my food wherever that human is hiding it."*

During all the years we have set up tent camps amidst the bears we have hunted, we have never once had a bear attempt to enter a tent or vehicle. All baits, all food containers and anything else (including toothpaste) that even remotely smells like something good to eat are sealed in plastic bags and stored on our tree platform. Despite this precaution, critters in black fur coats still come callin' now and then. Take my son John's bear:

John's Surprise

SNAP!

"What was that?" John whispered.

"Whatever it was, it was obviously big," I answered, "and it's out by our bait platform."

I poked my son, Dave, lying on a cot across the tent with earphones on, listening to the noon hour weather report. Dave swung his legs to the floor, asking, "What's up?"

"Shhh. You two get your rifles loaded and come with me. I think we've got a bear behind camp."

Fifteen minutes of careful stalking failed to reveal the cause of the twig-snap. Upon turning back toward camp, I thought of a similar mysterious sound outside a tent in the Yukon. A short time later, I found myself facing an enormous grizzly, towering over the dwarf arctic birches only 50 yards away.

"If it was a deer," I speculated, rounding our tent, "I think we would have heard it bounding away. John, while Dave and I bait his pit on the north ridge, I think you ought to stay here in camp. Keep your rifle loaded. I'm sure there's a bear hanging around."

Ten minutes later, Dave and I stopped mid-stride, bait-loaded sleds behind us.

"That shot was from camp," Dave hissed. "John got a bear!"

"Let's head back," I said excitedly, bounding toward the logging trail.

"Look at John jumping and waving," Dave bellowed, pointing east down the trail. "He's gotta bear all right."

"I really didn't think I'd actually see a bear," John explained between gasps. "I was just sitting in that lawn chair over there, reading a book. When I looked up to see if you guys had left the logging trail yet, there it was—50 yards away and heading right toward me. It was so close I was afraid to move. When I finally got my rifle up, I was so shaky that I knew I'd never be able to hit that bear. The bear wasn't paying any attention to me, so I eased of my chair laid down on my stomach, right there in that mud," he pointed.

"Then I didn't know what to do," John went on. "The bear was getting closer and I wasn't getting that broadside shot we're supposed to wait for. Finally, I aimed at a white spot on its chest. It looked like it was in line with its heart. At the shot, the bear did a back-flip and never moved again.

"I didn't know what was going to happen, being on the ground like that. I figured I'd be charged or something, but he never moved. I'm so excited that I haven't even gone over to look at the bear yet."

After a round of exuberant handshaking and back-slapping, we hung John's trophy 25 yards from where it dropped.

"Easiest bear drag I ever saw, " I said. "Maybe this is the way to hunt black bears, sitting on a chair in camp, readin' a book!"

During a couple of hunting seasons, bears regularly visited our camp at night, apparently attracted by our bait cache. Growing weary of the sounds of unrewarded midnight tree climbing (making it tough to sleep), I finally put a stop to it by hanging a lit Coleman lantern outside our tent. Nowadays, when bears around around at night, we switch on an electric yard light powered by an electric generator.

John and bear that came to camp.

Though a fearless dog might be an effective camp guard, I am reluctant to have one in bear camp. Not only might a dog result in over-kill —

causing bears to abandon the area — but I don't want to smell like a dog while I'm hunting.

Don't camp within 1/2–mile of a bait/stand site. Camping within 1/2-mile of a bait/stand site is likely to lead to abandonment of the site by all bears, abandonment by all but smaller bears or nocturnal feeding only.

Don't make uneccesary noises. Keep a low-profile. Bear camp is no place for loud shouting, loud radios, targeting firearms, grouse hunting or needlessly running ATVs. The greater your presence, the fewer bears you'll see, and the smaller they'll be. Worse, you may not see any at all. I've seen it happen. In one day or night, a noisy camp can easily ruin the effectiveness every bait/stand site within 1-2 miles.

Pre-Hunt Planning

Length of Hunt

Hunt 4-6 consecutive days. The odds for success are most favorable during the earlier days of the hunting season. As the season wears on, black bears become warier; less vulnerable to baiting. The number of days you should allow for hunting beginning with the opener depends somewhat on the size of the bear you'd like to harvest. If you have one with hind prints measuring 9 inches hitting a bait, it is wise to allow at least four days hunting time. Though a bruin this size may feed twice daily at a pit, because larger bears tend to be nocturnal, it typically takes 3-4 days to get a shot at one during daylight hours. Also, if a larger bear has abandoned a pit exhausted of food, it will probably not return for 3-4 days. It being prudent to move into bear country lodging a day early, and equally prudent to allow another day for breaking camp and taking care of a bear carcass, a six-day hunt is about the minimum when a trophy-class bear is the quarry.

The odds for taking a large bear are not very favorable when hunting weekends-only, especially when the do-it-yourselfer cannot take the time to re-bait midday, midweek. Each time re-baiting occurs on weekends-only, chances are it will take 3-4 days before a larger bear will return again after consuming the bait, meaning, the time and money spent hunting weekends-only will be most rewarding to the large bear.

Lesser bears invariably require less hunting time. If you're not fussy, you should be able to take a bear within the first 1-2 days. A minimum *any-legal-bear* hunt, then, should be at least four days long.

Plan to set up camp at least one day before hunting. There are several good reasons: 1) you'll be able to start from home at a more reasonable hour, driving at a more leisurely pace, 2) you'll have more time to make sure your camp is comfortable and bear-proof, 3) you'll be better prepared for hunting on the following day, getting a good night's sleep and having more time to make sure you haven't forgotten anything important, 4) you'll be better able to bait during favorable hours and 5) you'll have time to enjoy some of the other benefits of spending leisure time in the wilds.

If you leave early on the opener — early enough to bait midday — keep in mind that you may well take a bear that same evening. If you do, you may be in the woods — field dressing and dragging — until 10PM or later. Unless it is cold, you could then be faced with having to take an immediate trip to a registration station and locker plant (cooler). If you don't start out a day early, the odds are good (50-50) that you'll experience one of the most exhausting days in memory. Allow for every possibility. Try to make bear hunting leisurely, a time of bone fide recreation — not merely a quick, exhausting trip for bear meat.

Hunting Hours

Hunt afternoon and evening hours only. *Don't hunt in the morning.* If you attempt to sneak to a bait/stand site any time from two hours before sunrise until about 10AM, you will be almost certain to alarm one or more bears there. This can have a very dramatic, negative effect — causing abandonment of the pit or nocturnal feeding only. Except during high winds and/or moderate-to-heavy precipitation, it is virtually impossible for a human to stalk within effective shooting range of unsuspecting black bears. Their extraordinary hearing and sense of smell absolutely preclude that possibility. If you do get a shot, it will likely be from long range and the bear will probably be running through heavy cover — extremely risky under any circumstances. Don't take a chance. As anxious as you might be to at last put your sights on a bruin, assure your success by sleeping late in bear camp.

Plan to be in your stand by 2:30PM; 1PM if your bait pit is being visited by a large-to-very-large bruin. Before heading to your stand, give yourself at least an hour of preparation time — washing, changing clothes, applying camo, preparing gear, etc.

Plan to remain in your stand until sunset, or until an unwanted bear moves off far enough to enable you to leave without causing alarm.

Meals

Make breakfast your main meal of the day. Keep lunches light, especially when hauling bait. Also, keep fluid intake light midday so your bladder won't be distressed during that most productive period at the end of the day. Do not plan big meals at the end of the day, especially any that require significant preparation time. Chances are, you'll end up eating very late — after a bear has been brought into camp. Though everyone will be dying of thirst and hunger, no one will be inclined to spend much time cooking. Keep evening meals simple. Plan to eat quick and easy-to-prepare meals — sandwiches or pre-cooked foods that only require heating.

Baiting Hours

Bait between 10AM and 1PM. While it might be more ideal to bait midday on the day before the opener, baiting midday on the opener is unlikely to lead to any problems. After this final baiting before hunting begins, do not add bait to pits that yet contain more than a day's worth of food (with the exception of daily-used honey). Do not bait with smaller amounts daily. I've never known a pit to require more than 1-1/2 portions (225 pounds) of bait over the course of a six-day hunt.

Bear Carcass Preservation

Not being concerned about spoilage until a black bear is shot is an almost a certain way to insure spoilage. Well before opening day, the hunter should make all the arrangements necessary to make sure cooling of the hide and meat will quickly follow a successful kill.

Because hunters tend to treat black bear carcasses like the carcasses of white-tailed deer, (with apparent safety), because hunters fail to anticipate how difficult it can be to move the carcass of a black bear , and because so many fail to realize how quickly bear carcasses can spoil in weather typical of bear hunting seasons, untold numbers of black bears are needlessly wasted every season. It's a triple shame. To meaninglessly kill so magnificent an animal is wholly unethical. To waste so revered a trophy is unconscionable. To lose meat so astonishingly delicious is an unpardonable sin.

Make sure your bear meat and hide will be refrigerated within six hours or less (anticipating air temperatures ranging into the 50s and above).

To accomplish this, the hunter should first either pre-enlist the aid a dragging crew and/or plan to use of some kind of all-terrain vehicle that can get to a bear, towing it out on a sled or trailer.

How many men does it take to drag a bear? After dragging one any distance in the woods, most deer hunters will find it difficult to believe a 200-pound black bear only weighs 200 pounds. Such a bear will feel like it weighs closer to 300 pounds. There are a couple of reasons for this: 1) during bear hunting seasons the ground is not usually covered with slippery leaves or snow like during deer hunting seasons and 2) less streamlined black bear carcasses plow a much wider path than whitetail carcasses. Black bears will seem at least 1-1/2 to 2-times heavier than whitetails of the same weight. Generally, though one able-bodied man can drag a 150-pound yearling buck a considerable distance, the same hunter will have considerable difficulty dragging a 100-pound bear. Unless enlisted bear draggers are particularly strong men, it will usually take the following numbers of men to drag black bears of indicated weights:

Bear Weight (lbs.)	No. Draggers
150	2
200	3
300	4
400	5-6
500	7

Transporting a bear carcass from camp generally means the hunter will also need a pickup (truck) or trailer. Automobile trunks nowadays will hardly accommodate a bear weighing more than 300 pounds. Moreover, a car that has had a bear transported in its trunk will probably be chased by baying dogs for several weeks.

With an appropriate dragging crew on hand, lifting a larger bear into a pickup box or trailer will probably be no problem. With fewer than the required number of draggers, however, this can be a very challenging task. On more than a couple of occasions, I have had to winch a bear up into a tree or heavy tripod and then back my pickup underneath to get it loaded.

Since you will likely find yourself dragging your bear into camp during late evening in warm weather, it will also be important to find a butcher beforehand who will agree to hang your bear in a refrigerated room after normal business hours.

If you can't make such arrangements, upon registering your bear, you may be obliged to skin and cut your bear into chunks small enough to fit into coolers loaded with ice or a refrigerator. For this job, if bugs are bad or it's raining, a screen tent might come in handy. There's nothing like a fresh bear carcass for attracting clouds of night-stalking mosquitoes.

Ready At Last

All the necessary arrangements made, essential equipment ready to go, your shooting skills perfected, black bears agreeably accepting your offerings and the opener of the hunting season a day or two away, you are at last ready to go black bear hunting. Well, almost. Now it's time to learn the special tricks that will lead from camp to a photo of you beaming over a big black bear.

Chapter 6

Hunting Black Bears over Bait

From Camper/Baiter to Black Bear Hunter

Body and Clothing

In one hour you will head to a bait/stand site intending to shoot a large black bear. To insure everything will go as planned, now is the time to begin transforming yourself from an easy-to-smell, easy-to-see and easy-to-hear camper/baiter to a thoroughly-prepared, low-profile black bear hunter.

First, take a trip to the latrine. It is important to avoid having to leave your stand prematurely for this purpose.

If you use tobacco, consider this to be your last chance to smoke or chew until you return to camp.

Next, remove all unnatural odors from your body. In an area free of smoke (especially tobacco smoke), cooking odors and other strong, unnatural scents, use a wash basin filled with warm water, a washcloth, scentless soap and a scentless towel to cleanse your entire body, including your hair. Brush your teeth with baking soda. Do not use a deodorant, hair preparation, shaving cream or toothpaste. If you must shave, after softening your beard with warm water, use scentless soap as a shaving cream.

From this moment until you shoot a bear or return from your stand and change clothes, do not eat food, do not smoke or chew tobacco and do not chew gum. Drink water only. Stay away from cooking odors or anyone who is smoking tobacco.

Next, put on clean (odor-free) underwear (camo T-shirt) and socks. If your socks might become exposed while sitting in your stand, make sure they are of a color that will not be obvious to the eye.

Now get into your clean (odor-free) camo hunting clothing, including your camo belt with a non-glare buckle.

Stuff a camo handkerchief in a hip pocket. Aside from your billfold, hunting license and perhaps your compass (attached to your belt via a lanyard) and watch, that's about all you should carry in your pockets.

Boots

Slip on clean rubber boots. Do not wear leather boots under any circumstances. Leather boots are horrendous sources of strong, unnatural odors and there is nothing you can do to make them odorless for long, if at all. Do not wear fabric-type boots or shoes unless they have been washed in scentless soap and have not been worn since being washed.

Caution: if your rubber boots are shiny, take some time before the hunting season to thoroughly rub your boots with steel wool.

Headwear

Your camo hunting cap or hat should also be odor-free — not worn except when hunting. Like all other bear hunting clothing, do not wear a cap or hat that has not been previously washed with scentless soap. Caps or hats that cannot be washed are not acceptable for black bear hunting.

Standpack Gear

If you expect it to be cool at sundown, stuff a warm, odor-free camo jacket or sweater into your stand pack (small waterproof camo packsack). If rain is likely, tightly roll and tie your rainsuit — to reduce bulk and noise — before adding it to your pack.

In your stand pack, include anything you think is absolutely necessary for hunting, safety, navigation, survival, comfort and field dressing. Don't overload your pack with items not of immediate importance such as bear dragging equipment. Once you've shot a bear and, perhaps, recovered and field dressed it, return to camp to enlist aid and pick up whatever gear may be needed next, ridding yourself of gear no longer needed such as your weapon. For a list of gear I personally consider "essential" while hunting at a bait/stand site, see the underlined items in Chapter 4 under the subheading, "Black Bear Hunting Gear."

Whatever goes into your pack should not be allowed to rattle or emit unnatural odors. Wrapping and/or sealing noisy or odoriferous items in soft plastic bags generally solves these problems.

Applying Camo to Exposed Skin

The skin of the human face, neck, ears and hands is bright and shiny. It contrasts enormously against any background in the wilds. Though black bears have relatively poor vision, their eyes are adequate enough to easily identify an exposed human face within recommended stand-to-bait-pit distances, and then some. Older bears with significant human experience will rarely fail to identify even a motionless human face, skin exposed. Human hands, skin exposed, will also quickly attract the attention of a black bear. When motionless, camo dusts or pastes properly applied, or a camo mask or headnet and gloves, will provide the hunter with absolute protection against visual identification by all black bears within very short range (see color photo section).

As long as at least 90% of exposed skin is covered with irregular patches of varying colors appropriate to the hunter's tree stand background, it is doubtful any one camo pattern is superior to another. The main thing is to avoid missing large patches of skin. Most commonly missed are the neck (throat), ears, and areas about the eyes (including eyelids). When areas about the eyes are missed, wild animals seem to notice the human gaze more quickly, probably because the eyes appear larger. If exposed hair, mustache and beard are blond, gray (like mine) or white, apply camo colors to them as well.

Of the many products available for this purpose, I much prefer camo dust, colors applied with individual soft sponges. It is resistant to streaking in rain, it is completely non-reflective in sunlight (unlike many pastes) and it is easier to remove with soap and water.

I also prefer camo dust over camo masks and headnets. Masks and headnets obstruct my vision somewhat — my primary means of detecting approaching bears. The masks I've tried didn't work well when wearing eyeglasses — in cool weather they have the tendency to cause fog to form on my lenses at the very moment I'm taking aim. Nonetheless, a headnet is always accompanies me to my stands, ready for use when sun shines directly on my face (sun reflecting from my glasses) or when biting insects become unbearable.

Cover Scent

After all you've done to eliminate and protect your body and clothing from odors, using a notably strong-smelling substance like fox urine for bear hunting it might seem like a strange contradiction. There are a number of good reasons for using fox urine, however.

First, fox urine is a completely natural odor. Foxes are common wherever black bears live. Foxes routinely mark the bounds of their individual home ranges with their pungent urine. They not uncommonly steal meat portions from bait pits that have been opened by bears. A black bear, therefore, is not likely to be surprised by the smell of fox urine at or near a bait site.

Second, pungent fox urine seems to make it difficult, if not impossible, for keen-nosed animals like black bears and white-tailed to accurately judge the age of human trail scents that are not too fresh. Five to six hours after a hunter has passed, an older, more cautious black bear is much more likely to approach a bait pit after investigating the trail scents of a hunter whose boots are swabbed with fox urine than after investigating the trail scents of a hunter whose boots have not been swabbed with fox urine. Suppressing my trail scents with fox urine, I firmly believe, played a major role in providing me with the opportunity to take a Pope and Young bear last fall.

Third, pungent fox urine adds to the plethora of strong odors at a bait site that makes unavoidable human odors less significant (not obvious) to black bears. I have never observed any evidence that black bears are in the least intimidated by the smell of fox urine at a bait site, even when the smell originates from an elevated stand.

Fourth, when not feeding, black bears commonly bed safe distance away, usually within 200 yards downwind where they can monitor the scents and sounds of other animals near the pit, including other bears and humans. Black bears and whitetails pay considerable attention to the actions, sounds and scents of other creatures in their never-ending quest to avoid danger. Like whitetails, black bears seem to consider characteristically-wary foxes to be reliable sentinels of danger. I think black bears assume a human cannot be near a site where the odor of fresh fox urine suddenly permeates the air, even though airborne human odors may also be detected at the same time. No scent can completely cover human odors, not even skunk musk. *"That fox would simply not be urinating there if a human was near,"* a bear likely thinks. Airborne fox urine likely also makes a bedded black bear believe the sounds of a hunter approaching a stand, if subdued enough, are those of a fox.

Having discovered long ago that I can stalk at least twice as near a hidden, downwind deer or bear when my rubber boots are generously laced with fox urine, though my sinuses suffer, I use it routinely for hunting and photography, renewing it often when on foot.

Applying fox urine is usually one my last chores before heading to a stand. Using a swab (like used to apply liquid shoe polish) or a small, plastic-foam-type paint brush (kept in an air-tight plastic bag), I coat the entire foot portions of my rubber boots (another reason for using "rubber" boots). I apply plenty of fox urine. Early field testing indicated smaller amounts provide little or no benefits. If I must walk through water on the way to my stand, as soon as I gain dry footing again, I'll stop to re-apply fox urine.

Wanting the same advantages provided by fox urine going for me when leaving my stand, I again paint fresh fox urine on my boots before climbing to the ground. This precaution is taken to prevent unseen black bears from becoming aware of my unexpected presence at my bait/stand site late in the day. I don't want bears to start thinking it is unsafe to approach a bait pit except after dark.

To avoid filling your car, camp or cabin with the obnoxious odor of fox urine, when not hunting, seal your boots in a plastic bag (or two). The odor can be removed from your hands or boots by thorough washing with scentless soap and water.

Preparing Your Weapon

Ideally, for short-range bear hunting, your firearm or bow should not be shiny. It should be covered with flat (non-glare) camo — paint, tape or cloth (removable sock).

Your firearm or bow should not reek with the odors of grease, oil, solvent, fresh paint, fresh tape, glue (fresh arrow fetching), water-proofing or leather preservatives (a leather sling is not recommended). Before hunting, wipe your gun completely dry. Run a dry patch or two through the barrel. Camo should be applied 2-3 weeks early to effectively reduce or eliminate odors.

Your weapon must also be silent (until fired). Metallic rattles, squeaks or clicks are among the most ruinous sounds there are in bear or deer hunting. Black bears consider such sounds to be very dangerous. Don't overlook sling swivels. If necessary, quiet them with small strips of tape.

With a bear anywhere near, you must be able to operate your safety and/or cock your rifle without the least audible sound. It usually takes considerable practice (at home) to learn to accomplish this fete, but it must be done. It is virtually impossible to move a loudly clicking safety to the firing position and then get a shot off accurately before a black bear will respond (flee) — a black bear can react that quickly. Easing the safety forward without sound on my Ruger Model 77 is a real challenge. I must place my thumbs very firmly against both sides of the tang and then guide it forward very slowly in order to avoid it's normally horrendous "click." If you cannot do it without sound, use a different weapon.

Loading a cartridge into your firearm's chamber can also be a problem. This step, too, must be accomplished silently. Sure, you can load up before heading to your stand, but it is mighty risky to climb to your platform with a loaded firearm. It is equally risky to haul a loaded firearm up to your platform on a cord. Hunting accident reports are rife with accounts of hunters who have been shot by their own loaded firearms, whatever technique is used to get a weapon up into a tree. One hunter had his his pet semi-auto empty itself while dangling below on a string, the fifth shot plowing through his right foot. It is far safer to load up after you are settled in your stand. If you cannot load silently, either use a different firearm or resort to the noisy two-man approach to your stand, loading up before your partner noisily departs.

Generally, a well-seasoned bowhunter should have no problem using a bow silently up until the shot. To avoid the accidental clicking of an arrow shaft, a wide area surrounding the arrow rest should be covered with moleskin. The arrow rest, and perhaps the plunger, should also be padded. A very slow draw — requiring greater strength — will usually keep an arrow from emitting detectable sounds as it slides back over a rest and plunger. If you use a arrow holder, make sure it releases silently.

Should your weapon be loaded — a bullet chambered or an arrow strung — as you approach your stand? If you head in at the proper time, your chances of encountering a bear there — at least an older bear — are remote. Even if a bear was feeding there as you approach, except during high winds or moderate-to-heavy precipitation, it is extremely unlikely that you would succeed in getting close enough for a clean shot at any rate. If a bear was there, and you become aware of that fact before the bear discovers you, it would be best to back off and wait 30 minutes or so to avoid unnecessarily and fruitlessly alarming the bear. If it's the bear you want, alarm at this point could ruin your chances. Taking all factors into consideration, including having to unload before climbing to your stand, it's better to head in unloaded.

From Camp to Stand

The Direct Approach

When whitetail hunting, because it is commonly noisy underfoot, it is usually more effective to travel non-stop at a moderate pace to a stand, head pointed straight ahead. Whitetails tend to consider humans traveling in this manner to be harmless (non-threatening). Usually, they'll move to nearby cover, freeze until you have safely passed and then resume whatever they were doing. A human moving in a furtive manner — stopping often and peering about — will usually be considered dangerous, in which case encountered whitetails will leave the area, reducing considerably the effectiveness of the stand.

Black bears react to a hunter moving on foot in much the same way. The trouble with the direct approach, however, once you have reached your stand, every black bear within hearing will know your are there. If they don't hear you leave, younger bears may eventually work up the courage to approach your bait pit after a sufficient period of silence has elapsed, but older, wiser bears probably won't.

The Noisy, Two-Man Approach

The noisy two-man approach (talking softly all the way), one noisily departing (talking some more), is a commonly used alternative. It has the advantage of requiring no particular stalking skills. It is a preferred technique when re-baiting is necessary. Where bears have not been hunted over baits a great deal, this approach may fool a lot of bears, including an occasional large-to-very-large bear. Young bears are the most apt to be fooled. Sometimes they'll appear within 15 minutes after the noisy partner departs, excitedly expecting to find a fresh booty of bait. Where baiting is not uncommon, few older bears — if any — will be seen by hunters using this ruse less than 5-1/2 hours later.

The Silent Approach

When an older bear is the sole quarry and bait is adequate, I much prefer a stealthy, silent approach. Using this approach, I've seen more larger bears at bait/stand sites than when using any other method. For heavy, big-footed humans, unfortunately, such an undertaking is rarely easy. Though sound-muffling winds may be at maximum velocity between 1:00 and 2:30 PM and though during spring and early fall the forest floor may be soft and relatively quiet underfoot, the black bear's amazing sense of hearing considerably lessens these advantages. A successful, undetected approach is dependent on foresight, planning, preparation and skills adapted to three distinct parts of a bear bait/stand trail — the beginning, the middle and the end (the last 200 yards).

The Beginning Trail

Many hunters fail to realize older black bears readily recognize preludes to an impending approach by a human. For example, if an older bear hears a vehicle (or ATV) approach, hears it stop in the vicinity of the trail over which food is hauled in, and then hears a car door slam, it will rightfully expect to detect a human at the nearby bait site within a short period of time. Made extra alert by these sounds, it will be very difficult, if not impossible, for a human to move near without being detected. Even if the alerted bear does not detect the approaching hunter, imagine the effect. A vehicle that does not leave absolutely means a feared human is somewhere near. The bear has been conditioned to expect that. If the bear decides to approach the bait site later despite this knowledge, and it may not under these circumstances, it will be super cautious, ready to bolt upon detecting the least suspicious motion, sound or odor. In this case, fresh, airborne human scent will *not be ignored*, the bear wondering if the expected human somehow make its way to the bait pit without further sound; wondering further if that human is still there. If the vehicle has not departed, what else could the bear think? At best, it will be a spooky situation for the bear, one touched with peril. Under these circumstances a smart bear will not approach the bait pit until after dark, if at all.

When beginning your hike to your stand, therefore, either avoid using a noisy vehicle (or ATV) altogether, have someone drop you off and then drive away, or park your vehicle at least 1/2 mile from the beginning of your stand trail. From the outset, make no sounds that suggest a human is on the stand trail.

The Middle Trail

The middle section of your stand trail — that part between the beginning and a point about 200 yards (two football field lengths) short of your stand — can usually be safely traveled via the direct approach. Walk steadily — not fast, not slow, not stopping — consciously picking up your feet and putting them down lightly — no foot-dragging, no stumbling, no jumping and no heavy footfalls. Keep your head pointed straight ahead. If you have properly groomed your trail — removing freshly-fallen sticks and branches while hauling bait — there should be little danger of stepping on objects that will emit loud, identifying sounds. Keep your eyes on your trail to make sure. Don't step on logs — step over them. Don't push through intervening branches, allowing them to brush against your clothing, snatch your hat and then break or loudly swish. Stoop beneath branches or carefully raise them and then carefully let them down as you pass. Don't worry about bears and don't act as if

A nearby stream will make it tougher for bears to hear you.

hunting bears. On this section of the trail, your only concern should be "steady, silent, unerring passage."

The sounds of foliage and branches rustling in wind, the pattering of raindrops, the lapping of waves or the sounds of a rushing stream can very effectively screen the lesser sounds of a human approaching a bait pit. Take advantage of natural covering sounds whenever possible.

As you proceed, be on guard against triggering alarm among wild creatures along the way. Using the direct approach, unless directly in your path, most birds and animals will allow you to pass without alarm. If you encounter a creature in your path, stop, freeze and wait until it has moved a safe distance to one side. Do not stare directly at the bird or animal. This is particularly intimidating — the behavior of a predator keying on a prey — likely to trigger alarm. The sounds of a wildly flushing grouse, an angrily barking red squirrel or a snorting or bounding deer along your stand trail will be easily heard by a bear located within 1/2-mile of your bait pit. Such sounds — meaning something large, perhaps a dreaded man, is on the trail — put bears on alert.

The End Trail

Negotiating the last 200 yards of your stand trail without being identified as a human is critical to success when hunting all black bears, but more especially when hunting older bears.

Throughout this trail section you will likely tread well within the effective range of a black bear's sensitive nose, but, remarkably, the airborne human scents drifting downwind from your body are unlikely to trip you up. Moving cautiously and silently through this region, the mixture of pungent fox urine and carefully minimized human scent emanating from your body will identify you as a fox, not a human. Being conditioned to expect human odors at your bait/stand site, wayward human odors will not seem unusual, or intimidating, to a nearby bear.

Your greatest peril (to hunting success) along this section of trail will be self-made sounds uncharacteristic of foxes or, perhaps, a short-range encounter with one or more bears feeding at your bait pit.

Sounds That Identify Humans

When hunting black bears, the following are the sounds most likely to identify you:

1. Oral/nasal sounds — sneezes, snuffles, snorts, nose-blows, coughs, hiccups, throat-clearing, spitting, whistling, whispering and talking out loud.

2. Clothing (fabric) sounds — rough or hard fabric rubbing against fabric, rough or hard fabric rubbing against foliage, branches or tree bark, sounds of zippers, snaps or Velcro, and rustling of plastic or rubberized fabrics.

3. Foot sounds — heavy footsteps, rapid footsteps, foot dragging, jumping, tripping, falling, stomping, grating of boots, sounds of boots being drawn from mud, splashing through water, twigs or branches breaking loudly, twigs or branches breaking often and squeaky footwear.

Grouse and other wildlife met along a stand trail can ruin your chance for taking a larger bear.

4. Metallic sounds — rifle action or safety, loose (jingling or rattling) cartridges, coins, match safe, compass, buckle, keys, sling attachments, stand parts, tree steps, flashlight or flashlight batteries and ticking watch.

5. Wild sentinel alarm sounds — whitetail snort, foot-tapping or bounding, sounds (or sight) of rapidly fleeing animal of any kind, animal rapidly climbing tree, barking red squirrel, chipping chipmunk, scolding jay, chickadee or other bird, rapid caws of crow or raven and clucking or wildly flushing grouse.

6. Miscellaneous sounds — gun, bow or arrow striking branch, tree trunk or stand, objects dropped from stand, whittling, sawing, chopping or hammering and squeaks, grates or thumps of tree stand.

Foxes make none of the above sounds. Most are characteristically human-caused. Oh, sure, an unalarmed deer, moose or bear may step on and break twigs or branches (less audible and far less frequent than snaps caused by humans), but if a downwind black bear hears these sounds and smells only fox and human odors drifting from the vicinity of the sounds — not deer, not moose nor bear odors — what is a bear to think? What it is smelling can only be a fox or a human. If the sounds are human-like, not fox-like, the intruder can only be a human — not a noisy human hauling in food, but a skulking human, one that must therefore be considered *dangerous.*

Are black bears capable of such reasoning? Yes indeed. They may not think (reason) like humans, but when it come to matters of wilderness survival, the responses of older, experienced bears to sights, sounds and scents that suggest or identify human danger reflect very nimble and very intelligent brains.

If you earlier failed to carefully brush out this section of trail, failed to remove windfalls and fallen branches and failed to lay twin logs (nailed together so they won't roll) across mud and water, you're going to have a tough time trying to convince a nearby bear you sound like a fox. The most a bear should hear from you is subdued rustling of green grass or leaves as your near your stand. You must move slowly through this section, inspecting every patch of ground in your path before placing a foot on it. This takes total concentration.

A Bear at the Pit

Within this section, you must also proceed as if stalking a bear, which you may very well be doing. Though it is not likely that a bear will be feeding at your bait pit between 1:00 and 2:30PM, you can never be absolutely sure. It should not be your goal to stalk near enough for a shot, however. Such an attempt is almost certainly doomed to failure and it will likely result in abandonment of the bait pit (perhaps the entire area) by the bear involved.

I've only known two hunters who have managed to stalk near enough on foot for a decent shot at a black bear. One was a very experienced bear hunter who then shot a fine bear with his bow. I was the other, but the bear I might have considered large enough turned out to be a sow with twin cubs. After we all identified one another and cleared out, I never saw this trio of bears again.

As you near your stand, then, ease to a stop often, directing your eyes and ears on the vicinity of your bait pit 1-2 minutes (or longer) at a time. If a bear is there, when within 50 yards you might hear it moving about, moving logs, digging food out of the pit and/or eating — lapping food or chewing on bones — but don't count on it. You can't be absolutely sure until you've had a chance to visually check the pit area (from a distance) for a period of 1-2 minutes.

If you hear or see a bear at your pit, cautiously back away making no sounds. Do your best to avoid alarming the bear. Once sure you cannot be seen by the bear, carefully and slowly tiptoe back along your stand trail until at least 100 yards away. Then move off-trail about 25 yards or so, downwind. There, sit motionless on a log in good cover for about 30 minutes, facing your stand trail. The bear may use your trail when it leaves.

After about 30 minutes has passed or about 15 minutes since the bear ambled past, try again, moving forward with the utmost caution and stealth. Though most bears will feed and depart within 30 minutes, sometimes one will remain at or near a bait pit 1-2 hours. A black bear might nap within a flattened nest-like area in deep cover within a few yards. Consider all possibilities before striding openly to your stand.

Within that final 50 yards, it is quite natural to experience an eerie feeling inside. There is no danger at this point, however, certainly nothing like the threat that looms from ten-foot willows surrounding a grizzly kill.

Only once during all the years I have hunted bears over bait have I found myself within short range of black bears — the sow and cubs mentioned above — while approaching a bait pit. At the moment I realized the unsuspecting bear feeding 30 yards before me (about 250 pounds) had twin cubs — both enjoying themselves climbing in an adjacent tree — I indeed felt I was in grave danger. Stifling the urge to flee or climb a tree, I instead froze, curious. Within 30 seconds the sow spotted me, her gaze directed by the cubs who were staring inquisitively from tree branches about six feet above. The sow uttered a soft but sharp woof. The cubs immediately scrambled to the sow's rear. She then turned and led her wards away, gathering speed as they plunged into thick balsams opposite the bait pit. If you're cautious as you approach your stand — not bursting into the bait pit clearing without first checking it from a distance — this is about the worst you might expect from bears caught feeding.

If you should unexpectedly blunder into a bear within short range anywhere along your stand trail, do not immediately turn tail and flee. Though it is extremely unlikely any black bear will pursue you, instant flight may invite pursuit, just as fleeing from a barking dog may trigger pursuit. No matter how large the bear, stand your ground facing the bear. Being a tall, erect and feared human, you'll present an imposing, intimidating figure, one of great danger. Give the bear time to get over its initial shock and think about it. If the bear is not one you'd care to shoot and it does not soon retreat, talk to it quietly. Do not challenge it by moving forward or throwing things at it, invoking rage or panic. If the bear does not soon depart (keep in mind it may have a cub hidden nearby), back slowly away, all the while facing the bear. When finally out of sight, turn and walk quietly away (along your trail) until at least 100 yards away.

Move off-trail, downwind, and wait 30 minutes before returning toward your stand. Whatever you do, once out of sight of a bear, it is generally unnecessary to sprint to your vehicle or camp.

From Stand Trail to Stand Platform

Upon arriving at my bait/stand site, two quick chores precede climbing to to my elevated platform: 1) set out a bear lure and 2) prepare to haul my bow (or firearm) to my platform.

Using a Bear Lure

An increasing number of potions are making their way to sporting goods shelves these days and each, of course, is reputed to be the *ultimate* bear lure. Of the commercial preparations I've tried, including black bear urine, I've had limited or no success. That doesn't mean I don't recommend using a commercial lure, nor does it mean commercial bear lures don't work. I'm sure some do.

The lure I use is not generally regarded as a lure — *honey*. No matter what foods, odors or so-called "lures" I have ever personally tried, nothing has ever out-lured honey. Honey is the first thing a bear will head for upon arriving at one of my bait pits. Honey is the only lure I know of that might attract a strictly nocturnal bear to a bait-site during legal shooting hours. Being as reliable as it is, I treat honey as a bone fide bear lure, using it only when hunting, straight from the bottle or burned.

Having discovered one cup of honey is as effective as a quart, that's all I routinely take to to a bait site. To position a bear at the exact spot where I'd to shoot it, I normally dribble honey widely over the logs covering my bait pit , even if the logs have been previously moved by bears.

P & Y Bear taken by Todd Sturgul using methods described in this book.

If it is raining, or rain is expected, I'll pour honey widely over the rough bark of a mature tree (one-with sheltering branches) standing near the pit.

Honey Burn

Though the "honey burn" is a widely touted method of attracting black bears, I use it only as a last resort. If it was illegal to bait before the opener, I'd burn honey daily until I had bears hitting baits. A honey burn is one of the quickest ways there is to lure bears to a new bait site. To work, of course, a burn must be located upwind of a bear. If it doesn't work, one can assume there are no bears downwind.

My favorite way to burn honey is as follows:

1. Dump one cup (or more) of honey into an open 2-pound coffee can.

2. Insert this can into an open 3-pound coffee can containing 6-8 glowing charcoal briquettes. The charcoal can should have air holes punched around its base and a long, wire bail attached to the top so the cooker can be hung from a branch off the ground. I usually start the charcoal burning (in its can) at the bait site, using crumpled newspaper as a starter. As soon as the charcoal starts burning — glowing white patches appearing — I insert the honey can and hang the cooker from a stout branch.

The honey will begin bubbling in 20-30 minutes, emitting a sweet, pungent odor. Burnt-honey smoke will begin billowing from the cooker in about 60 minutes. One cup of honey will usually produce strong bear-attracting odors 2-3 hours.

The effective downwind range of a honey burn is 1/4-1/2 mile, depending on wind velocity. Stronger winds hold the odor near to the ground over greater distances. Some bears will waste no time moving toward the smell of burning honey, whatever the time of day. Honey burns are most effective during periods when bears are most active — early and late in the day.

Keep two precautions in mind when using a honey burn: 1) do not bang cans together (or make any other unnatural sounds) when carrying and setting up a honey cooker at a stand site (pad parts with crumpled newspaper) and 2) never leave burning honey untended (take your cooker with you when departing).

The smell of burning honey will draw bears $1/4 - 1/2$ mile downwind.

Preparing a Weapon for Hauling Up to a Stand

Whatever system you use to get your weapon up to an elevated tree stand, at no time in your career as a big game hunter are you in greater danger of being injured by your own weapon. At no time is the accuracy of your weapon in greater jeopardy. At no time are you more likely to be identified by a bear because of sounds made by your weapon. I've tried everything. Nothing is safer than hauling an *unloaded* weapon up from the ground via a stout cord — *after* you have climbed to your platform.

When climbing, a rifle or bow carried in any way will invariably snag on a branch and/or bang against your stand tree, a step or your stand. One unnatural sound of this kind is all it takes to ruin your chance to take a large bear (or large white-tailed buck).

Climbing with a loaded rifle (or bow) on your back is foolhardy. I was once nearly shot by a loaded rifle being carried on a sling. Kneeling, while pushing through thick hazels, the safety was snagged and then the trigger of a rifle being carried on the back of a hunter behind me. The bullet burned the left side of my neck. I've been jumpy about rifles casually carried on slings ever since.

Before climbing, place your unloaded (no bullet chambered, all arrows quivered) weapon on the ground beneath one edge of your stand. Lay it where it will not swing or snag a branch as you draw it up (something extra to think about when preparing your stand).

I usually tie one end of my 20-foot haul cord twice about the tip of the upper limb of my bow. This keeps my arrow fletchings from being snagged and damaged as I raise my bow. When using a rifle, I loop one end of my cord twice about my rifle's pistol grip and tie it securely — **never passing it through the trigger guard**. The bore will then hang safely downward as I raise my rifle. The other end of my cord is then tied to a belt loop at one side of my waist.

Climbing to a Stand Platform

When climbing, one errant sound can ruin all your good work. When preparing your stand, then, give yourself every chance to climb safely and silently — no squeaks, no cracks, no thumps, no grunts and no grating of clothing, backpack or boots. Save all the silhouette-hiding branches you can (all the way to the ground), but make sure you can get to your platform without struggle or racket.

Where stout branches are not handy, I position screw-in steps about 18 inches apart (when using a portable stand) — a comfortable distance between steps for me. Wearing soft gloves, I arch my body away from the tree as I climb, watching my feet. If I don't watch my feet, I'll sometimes miss steps, and upon missing a step, I'm likely to noisily grate a boot against the tree trunk below, groping for a foot hold.

My final step to my stand platform is taken with utmost caution. When unused for several weeks, a portable may lurch with a squeak, groan or rattle when weight is suddenly applied. When preparing my stand, therefore, I make a special point of providing myself with a high handhold — a screw-in step or branch — from which I can support my weight as I gently ease onto my platform.

Buckling Up

No matter how experienced you are at stand hunting, and no matter what kind of an elevated stand you use, upon stepping onto your stand platform and removing and hanging up your backpack, securely fasten yourself to your stand tree with a sturdy safety belt (don't use a rope). Remember, it's going to get mighty exciting up there, so much so that you should not trust your body to keep you from falling from your stand. Hitch the tree end of your safety belt low above your stand seat. Give yourself just enough slack to be able to turn from side-to-side while seated without rubbing your back (clothing) against your stand tree.

Hauling Up a Weapon

Untie your haul cord from your belt loop and hitch it to something — a handy branch or stand part — out of the way. If your bow or rifle becomes snagged on a branch as you raise it, don't try to force it free by jerking on your cord. Rather than chance making undue noise or ruin the accuracy of your weapon, climb down and set things right. Raise your weapon slowly, keeping your eyes on its progress all the way up. Once up, lay your weapon across your lap. Untie your cord, coil it up and lay it out-of-the-way beneath your seat, ready for use when it is time to lower your weapon to the ground.

Preparing for a Long Vigil

Sitting fully alert up to six hours in an elevated stand without making detectable motions or sounds is probably the toughest part of black bear hunting. After 2-3 hours of it, stand hunting becomes mental and physical agony. Having suffered through three decades of sitting long hours in trees — hunting, studying and photographing whitetails (more than 4000 hours from August, 1986 to April, 1987) — I've learned some tricks that make stand hunting more tolerable. They are as follows:

Before hunting, get a good night's sleep. It's particularly tough to be an effective stand hunter when you're nodding off. When physically exhausted, not only will you soon become easy to spot — frequently yawning, stretching, standing up, and otherwise moving about — but you could even fall asleep — snoring and/or suddenly finding yourself thrashing at the end of your safety belt. Worse, in the event you do not somehow alarm your expected quarry long before it draws near, you may suddenly open your eyes and find yourself starring at a bruin ready to flee at the blink of an eye. You can't win in this situation. Plenty of sleep is a vital step toward success in black bear hunting.

Eat and drink lightly before hunting. Not only will you be less logy, you'll be less apt to feel the need for a latrine before the day is over.

Make sure your stand seat is well padded. If all or part of your seat is firm to start with, within a few hours of sitting an important part of your anatomy will feel bruised, making you fidgety. There is absolutely nothing wrong with toting to your stand (in your standpack) a soft pillow to sit on. It should be covered with a soft (quiet), camo fabric.

Periodically change your sitting position. Every 30 minutes or so, switch from an upright position to a slouch, then to a quartering position facing slightly to the right, and then to the left.

Remaining seated, periodically straighten, flex or tighten muscle groups in your legs, arms, neck and back. This will greatly forestall or ease stiffness and high-profile thrashing, stretching or standing. Stretch your legs by slowly extending them out beyond the front edge of your stand platform.

Chew on something (something that does not emit an unnatural odor — not chewing gum or chewing tobacco). When you feel the need to do something physical — feeling fidgety — cut a small, green twig from a nearby branch and stick it in your mouth like a toothpick. Fiddling with such a stick, using your lips and tongue only, does a remarkable job of stifling a fidgety body.

Keep your mind occupied. A tree stand in the wilderness is a wonderful place to solve life's mysteries. It's also a wonderful place to enjoy Nature's world — flora and fauna. To stave off boredom in a lonely tree stand, I like to match sounds with the creatures that make them; to watch the antics of songbirds, grouse, owls, porcupines, weasels, scurrying mice, deer — whatever wild creature happens along. When hunting bears, however, do not occupy your mind so completely (reading a book, for example) that you fail to notice when a bear is approaching.

Preparing a Firearm for the Shot

When using a firearm, loading a round into the chamber undetected (making no obvious, metallic sounds) will be a serious challenge. Using a semi-automatic, this will probably be impossible — the bolt being required to slam shut to properly chamber a round. Moving very slowly, you should be able to load a lever, pump or bolt action rifle without sound. Gently open the bolt about half-way, carefully feed a round into the chamber, by hand rather than feeding one up from the magazine, and then ease the bolt forward until firmly locked — lever tightly up, pump firmly forward or bolt handle firmly down. Once a live round is chambered, silently engage your rifle's safety. Never neglect to keep the safety "on" until you know you will soon fire at a bear. After hours of boredom, you never know when you might absentmindedly put pressure on the trigger. It would be a shame to ruin your hunt by accidentally discharging your firearm.

Once settled in your stand, rehearse in your mind the steps you must take before you will be able to fire at a bear. Imagine how it will be with a black bear feeding only 10 yards before you. Now slowly raise your weapon and take aim (using a rest) at a knot on one of the logs covering your bait pit. Ask yourself how you might do it better, making whatever adjustments are necessary. Take note of perils in your movement, positions in which your rifle or bow swings near objects that would make a loud noise if brushed or bumped.

With such practice, it should at once become obvious that the less you have to do — the less you have to move — when preparing to fire, the more likely it is that you will succeed. This means your rifle or bow should be in your hands, across your lap, ready to raise at all times. At least one thumb or finger should constantly lie near your rifle's safety, ready to make that first discreet step toward firing. Don't hang your weapon on a branch or prop it in some kind of holder. Don't add to the difficulty and the amount of motion needed to prepare for the shot.

Preparing Archery Gear for the Shot

If you are a bowhunter, after attaching your arm guard, lay your bow across your lap — your broadhead-tipped arrow nocked and lying across your arrow rest. Keep your left hand on or very near your bow's grip, your right hand on or very near the nock of your arrow. If you use a mechanical release, it is best to keep it hooked to your string. Doing this, not only will your bow be less likely to slip from your lap, but you will never find it necessary to make a far-reaching movement (likely to be quick and easy to spot) toward your bow when a bear suddenly appears.

Preparing Other Gear

Whatever else you might need during your long vigil should be close at hand in your standpack. Your pack, its cover unzipped or unsnapped, should hang within a short grasp, but not where it might interfere with your shot.

Other common concerns when sitting long hours in a tree stand are rain, cooling temperatures, direct (in the face) sunlight and biting insects.

Rain

If rain is in the forecast, don't wear your rainsuit until it becomes necessary. Rainsuits are made of noisy, shiny fabrics. Unless it is actually raining — raindrops noisily pattering down — the grating whisper of rainsuit fabric will easily spook a black bear within 50-75 yards.

Cooling Temperatures

Cool evenings are common when hunting black bears. Make use of warmer clothing when temperatures are cool, but don't wear clothing any warmer than is necessary while traveling to your stand during the heat of the day. If you do, you'll sweat. If you sweat, odor-causing bacteria will quickly spoil your attempts to remain odor-free. Carry warmer clothing in your stand pack. Don't pull it on until until you notice it is becoming a bit too cool for comfort.

In northern regions where I generally hunt, a camo chamois shirt or a medium-weight sweater, knitted or jersey, is usually adequate. My absolute favorite cool weather bear hunting garb is a camo, fleece-lined, hooded sweatshirt with a full nylon zipper closure (I rarely use the zipper). Not only will this sweatshirt keep me cozy in temperatures well into the low 20s, but the fabric is not bulky and extremely quiet. On days that start out cool, I'll don light, cotton long-johns and heavier socks before heading to my stand, hiking slowly, then, to avoid sweating.

Direct Sunlight

When spotlighted by direct rays of the sun, your body, weapon, stand and any movements you make will become much more likely to be spotted and identified by wary black bears. When caught in this unfortunate situation — usually temporary — it is extremely important that nothing on or about you is shiny (reflects sunlight). Always avoiding the use of reflective surfaces when hunting any big game, the only hazardous items I must deal with in a bear stand are the lenses of my eyeglasses and rifle scope (highly reflective) and the fabric of my rainsuit (somewhat reflective). My rainsuit is therefore never worn in bright sunlight.

To prevent reflections from my eyeglasses (including sunglasses), I make a point of using mature evergreens as stand trees. Their drooping branches cast protective shadows. I also make sure my stands never face the setting sun — west. This is usually enough to keep sunlight away from the lenses of my rifle scope as well.

Of course, it isn't always practical, or possible, to eliminate the west from your field of vision. Realizing black bears approach from the west at least 25% of the time and knowing reflections from my glasses have frightened off black bears in the past, I never hunt without being prepared to deal with the rays of the setting sun. Most of the time I simply wear a hat or cap with the brim or visor pulled down low, cocked to one side or a portion cut out to accommodate my bowstring at full draw. If when in my stand I can see I'm going to have problem with the sun despite all these precautions, I'll pull on a camo headnet. Though a headnet will reduce vision somewhat, it will provide absolute protection against eyeglass reflections. To make sure I will shoot well when wearing a headnet, I commonly wear one when at the practice range.

Biting Insects

Mosquitos, gnats, no-see-ums, flies, chiggers, ticks, bees, hornets, wasps and yellowjackets are facts of life when hunting black bears over bait, especially when the weather is warm. The odors characteristic of bait pits attract flying insects in droves. I have never been driven from a stand by any insects, but I've come close. For one reason or another, mosquitos are at their worst when black bears are most active. Having suffered under unusual onslaughts by mosquitos while a bear is before me, I never head to stand without being well-prepared for them.

My first line of defense is insect-resistant clothing — thick or tough enough to ward off stings or bites. When necessary, I'll use my headnet to protect my face and gloves to protect my hands. Using a mechanical arrow release, bound to my wrist with a Velcro band, it doesn't matter how thick my gloves are when bowhunting. When insects become particularly bloodthirsty, I'll slip on my 100% bite-proof, camo rainsuit.

No matter how "natural" an insect repellant may smell to a human, all are loaded with bear-repelling odors. I use a rub-on (never a spray) repellant only as a "last resort." When the use of a repellant is anticipated — hordes of biting insects being regularly met when baiting — it would be prudent to condition your bears to the odor(s). To prevent bears from being spooked by a repellant when hunting, douse yourself with the same repellant while baiting, even depositing a bit on something near bait pits with each baiting. If you neglect to take this precaution, or if someone else does your baiting, do not use a repellant when hunting.

Detecting Approaching Black Bears

When hunting black bears from a tree stand, rarely will you get much of an advance warning when one is approaching. A scolding red squirrel or jay might signal the approach of a bear, but rarely will you hear a bear step a on snapping twig or branch. Only occasionally might your hear a bear bawl — likely a cub. Only twice in twenty years have I heard a nearby black bear threaten another with a throaty woof. Only three times during that period have I heard a nearby bear chase another.

Nine times out of ten, you probably won't know a bear is near until you actually see one, and then probably not until it is well within 50 yards. Like silent puffs of smoke, black bears ease effortlessly through seemingly impregnable cover with remarkable grace and deceptive speed. It almost seems as if they walk an inch or two above the ground, paws supported by cushions of air. This is likely due to fact that they have sensitive, human-like soles on their feet, making it possibly to avoid bearing down on objects that might emit significant sounds. Never count on having plenty of opportunity to get ready for the shot before a black bear is very near. Chances are, you won't have the opportunity to even begin raising your weapon until your quarry has spent some time feeding at your bait pit.

You must depend almost wholly on your eyes to detect the approach of a black bear. Nonetheless, never attempt to maintain a constant visual surveillance of the entire area about your stand. Keep your head pointed toward one side of your bait pit. Move your eyes only, keying mostly on the cover downwind of your stand. A bear is most apt to approach from that direction, using the wind to check the pit area for danger before approaching nearer. Don't count on it, however. Older bears, especially, may start out from downwind, but then widely circle your stand before coming in. You may spot a bear doing this, and you may not. Once an older bear has circled your stand, it may approach from any direction. It may approach along your stand trail. It may approach from directly behind you, your first glimpse being a wide, black specter emerging from directly beneath your stand platform.

If you are craning your neck, attempting to keep an eye on the entire area about your stand, chances are you'll be spotted, and likely without your knowledge. Keep in mind black bears often look up into trees when approaching a bait pit. More than likely, a bear near your pit will gaze directly at you at least 2-3 times before you can fire your shot. When well-camouflaged and motionless, it is very unlikely any black bear will identify you, even when staring at you from a distance of a few yards. Black bears quickly spot movements, however. Upon spotting the movement of something large in a tree that is obviously not another black bear, black bears very abruptly melt into thick cover, likely to be never seen again.

Forget the area behind you then. Survey it only with your ears. If you hear something — the swish of grass, the soft snap of a twig or a barking red squirrel, for example — assume a bear is approaching, but do not move — not even slowly — until either the cause of the sound(s) is within your field of vision, its head pointed in a safe direction, or 15 minutes have passed without detecting another suggestive sound.

With slowly roving eyes, give only the area before you your best effort. Accept the fact that a bear may suddenly appear without warning from directly beneath your stand. That distinct possibility should never be a major concern. A bear beneath your stand has only one thing in mind — to safely enjoy the goodies you've provided. Be patient. Don't move. Keep your breathing light and normal. The hungry bear will soon move to the bait pit, freeing you to prepare for your shot.

How Black Bears Approach Bait Pits

Cubs yet under the tutelage and protection of maternal sows often rush to bait pits well ahead of their mothers, demonstrating little caution. When you see one or more smaller bears behave in this manner, expect soon the appearance of a disgruntled sow. The sow will probably make a quick survey of the area before settling down to feed.

Young, subadult bears — 1-1/2 – 3-1/2 years of age — are often the first (earliest) bears of the afternoon to appear at a bait pit that is being visited by multiple bears, older and progressively more dominant bears appearing later and later. Younger bears approach cautiously, spending several minutes silently standing in dense cover, usually downwind, to intently size up the area via sight, hearing and smell before exposing themselves in the bait pit clearing. Such bears act as if greatly concerned for their safety, being inordinately alert to sounds suggestive of danger and constantly poised to flee. This nervousness is not likely due to human threat. Rather, it seems most to arise from the threat of attack by older, more dominant bears. Younger bears will feed quickly and depart within 15-30 minutes when older bears are visiting the same bait pit. Sometimes two young adult bears of equal or nearly equal size will approach together or nearly together, carrying foods and eating at opposite sides of the bait pit clearing.

Sometimes the progression of bears is reversed. When two or more adult bears of various ages are in the vicinity of a bait pit (black bears know it), those less dominant will sometimes merely pass through a bait pit clearing early without pausing. Hardy breaking stride, one might snatch up a loose morsel of bait and carry it away. When such bear behavior is noted, the hunter can be certain a larger bear will soon approach the pit. This happened at my son-in-law's stand on opening day last September.

Kevin's Lost Arrow

When I emerged into our bear camp clearing on opening day last fall, darkness closing in fast, something seemed amiss. My son, Dave, wasn't there yet, but the Stones were — Kevin and my oldest daughter, Peggy. Usually a bubbly couple, they were standing near my truck, not saying a word.

"Well?" I presently asked.

"Lost an arrow," Kevin answered solemnly. Peggy began to grin.

"Okay, I'll bite," I said, suddenly knowing what Kevin was going to say. "How did you lose an arrow?"

"It's in a bear," he answered, "over by the beaver pond!"

With this announcement, the floodgates opened. "I saw *three*," he started excitedly. "The first one came in about six, but it didn't stop. Before I could get my bow up, it was gone, heading east. About fifteen minutes later, a slightly bigger one appeared, coming in from the west just like the first bear. Then without breaking stride, it grabbed a small chunk of meat and continued east.

"I was starting to wonder what I was doing wrong. Here I had two bears within five yards and couldn't get a shot at either one. Then I started to think there might be a bigger one nearby, maybe making those first bears nervous about about being near my pit. Then, sure enough, here came a third bear, bigger than the others, following the exact same path.

"This one stayed. The trouble was, after grabbing a chunk of meat, it laid down on the undisturbed logs over my pit — not lying lengthwise, but across them, facing me! I had to freeze at least fifteen minutes, not daring to blink or even take a normal breath.

"When the bear finally got up and turned, standing quartering away, it was easy. I couldn't miss! The arrow hit the bear with a slapping sound. With that, it bounded southeast, right into the worst tangle of beaver cuttings you ever saw.

"After waiting ten minutes, I climbed down and marked its trail. It's a nice boar. It only went 35 yards.

"A perfect heart shot!" Kevin added, rightfully beaming.

When winds are calm to light (5 mph), younger adult bears will usually being feeding 2-3 hours before sunset. Commonly bedding very near bait pits, these are the bears most likely to appear within 15-30 minutes after fresh bait has been provided (whatever the time of day).

As explained earlier, older boars (and sometimes older sows) tend to be frustratingly tentative and extremely cautious when approaching a bait pit. Some old boars absolutely refuse to approach bait pits during daylight hours. Quite commonly, especially where baiting has been going on for two or more years, older boars will widely circle bait pits to assess the age of human scents on bait/stand trails before deciding whether to approach the sequestered food or not. The fact that few hunters head for their bear stands early enough (six hours before sunset) is one of the main reasons few black bears 5-1/2 years of age or older are seen by hunters, much less harvested.

A bait pit that is being regularly hit by a bear, but is not visited by one or more younger bears 1-3 hours before sunset, is very likely the possession of a large and dominant boar. Such bears are so feared by younger bears, including sows with young, that none dare visit a bait pit from which the hair-triggered titan's intimidating scents originate.

Avoiding a Black Bear's Sixth Sense

Almost every living creature, including man, eventually senses when it is being stared at by a potentially dangerous creature. White-tailed deer sense it quickly; black bears even more quickly. It matters little whether a black bear can identify the staring, thus intimidating, creature. Once noticed, if the eyes continue to stare — tracking it's movements — much more than 15-30 seconds, the bear, whatever its size, will suddenly turn and flee. As soon as a bear is spotted in the vicinity of a bait/stand site, therefore, the hunter should make every effort to avoid direct eye contact for more than a few seconds. Except when aiming your weapon, keep your head deliberately pointed to one side. Size up your quarry and keep track of its movements via peripheral vision only.

The Shot

At last satisfied no danger lurks in the vicinity of the bait pit, the bear eases into the clearing from thick, back-tall ferns and heads directly toward the irresistible honey festooning the logs lying over its familiar treasure of tantalizing foods. Taking one last glance about the clearing — little noting the leafy mass on the regularly-seen platform 12 feet up in the adjacent tree — the bear lowers its massive head and begins noisily lapping honey.

All those weeks of work, months actually, are about to pay off. The vision that has long haunted your mind is finally real — a sure-enough, braggin'-sized, unsuspecting black bear is standing only ten paces from the base of your stand tree.

The trouble is, your heart is thumping like never before, your mouth feels like it's filled with cotton, your knees and hands are trembling, the hair on the back of your neck is standing on end and you're wet with perspiration. This bear before you is obviously a swift and powerful monster — one with awesome claws and fangs. *Oh Lord,* you're thinking, *what made me want to do this? If I goof, this animal could make mincemeat out of me in seconds!*

Welcome to bear hunting, my friend. What you feel at this moment has been felt by all bear hunters since time immemorial. Dan'l Boone felt it. Davy Crockett felt it. I've felt it. It never changes. It's natural. It's even good. It's the best motive there is for wanting fervently to do what you must do next — make a *perfect* shot. Make that *perfect* shot by adhering to the following rules:

1. Don't rush your shot. It is only natural (human) to feel the urge to throw up your weapon and fire as quickly as possible. It's like the urgency you feel when hooking a big fish — you want to get it into the boat as quickly as possible. That's a dumb thing to do, of course. With a big one on the line, you must take your time, concentrating on keeping the fish from breaking the line, not even attempting to boat it until the time is right. Think of that bear down there as being a big fish. It will be necessary to play a bit before you can succeed in bringing it to net.

At this point, black bear hunting over bait is very different from whitetail hunting. With whitetails, as you probably know, golden opportunities for perfect shots are uncommon and fleeting. With a black bear feeding before you, only one fleeting, golden opportunity to fire is extremely rare — you'll actually have dozens of perfect chances and they'll be spread out over a period of at least 30 minutes. There is absolutely no need, then, to rush your shot. In fact, to make a perfect bear shot, you can't rush your shot. As golden opportunities — perfect shot angles — come and go while you are slowly raising your weapon, don't despair. If you don't alarm the bear, there'll be more golden opportunities; plenty more. If you do alarm the bear — detectable motions being the most likely culprit — there'll be no golden opportunities; none whatsoever.

2. Raise your weapon more slowly than you've ever raised it before. Never under-estimate the visual capabilities of a black bear. When a black bear is at your bait pit, every motion you make must be smooth and "ultra-slow". How slow is "ultra-slow?" If you move fast enough get your weapon ready to fire in less than two minutes, the bear will likely spot you.

It's not easy to spend two minutes or more raising any weapon. Try it well before the opener. If it's tough to do, your arm muscles giving out in less than two minutes, practice this essential bear hunting skill until it is well mastered.

3. Freeze whenever your quarry's head is pointed in your direction. Chances are, from the moment you begin to raise your weapon until the moment you can finally fire, more than five minutes will have elapsed, maybe even 15 minutes. The reason is, it is commonly necessary to freeze — completely halt all motions — each time a black bear is faces you.

Having predator eyes situated on the front of its head, a black bear's field of vision is much like that of a human. Moving your hands about your head, eyes pointed straight ahead, you can determine for yourself where a black bear's "blind zone" is — the area in which motion cannot be spotted. It will be slightly wider than a half-circle (about 190 degrees) on a horizontal plane and slightly narrower than a half-circle (about 170 degrees) on a vertical plane This means you are only completely safe from being spotted when a black bear's head is facing away — quartering or fully away. To put it another way, when you can see a bear's eyes, it can discern any obvious motions you make. Whenever a bear faces you then, you must cease all movements.

The trouble is, black bears never completely relax their caution. The least sound suggestive of danger, perhaps merely caused by wind in a tree, a scurrying squirrel or another approaching bear, will cause a feeding black bear to suddenly turn and freeze, intently staring, listening and sniffing. Not uncommonly in this situation, one will rise up on hind paws, fully erect, to make better use of its eyes. Under such scrutiny, there is probably not a moving creature within 200 yards that can avoid being identified by a black bear.

It being impossible to foretell when a black bear may suddenly become alerted by a sound, the hunter must be constantly poised — alerted via peripheral vision — to assume a "bear-vision-proof freeze". What is a "bear-vision-proof freeze"? A *complete* lack of motion. Caught in the middle of the act of raising your weapon, an effective freeze can become downright punishing. You must instantly stop raising your weapon, wherever it is situated, you must avoid blinking your eyes, and you must avoid rapid or obvious chest movements, breathing lightly — taking in and easing out small breaths of air. It's punishing, but, fortunately, black bears do not usually spend more than 15-60 seconds studying areas from which potentially dangerous sounds originate. Once a bear is satisfied and resumes feeding — its eyes turned away — you can also resume what you were doing.

If a black bear faces you while feeding, however, you must remain frozen until it turns away. Stuck with a bear facing me while feeding at a bait pit one evening last fall, I had to suffer the agony of a total freeze that lasted 15 minutes. After about 10 minutes, I was praying for divine intervention, but I made it.

4. Forget the bear — concentrate on what you are doing until ready to shoot. Throughout the ordeal of getting ready to shoot, you must not make a sound. Avoiding detection by a black bear's ears during this process will be your greatest challenge. To make absolutely certain you will not make an alarming sound, you must turn your attention to yourself, carefully monitoring your every movement.

If using a rifle, your first significant peril will be your rifle's safety. Mine being difficult to move without sound, it was always my goal to move my safety well before a bear was near. Regularly failing on this score, my next goal was to move my safety during the exact moment a bear opened my bait pit, clattering logs being counted on to mask any sound my safety might accidently make. That worked, but more often I was faced with the prospect of moving my safety in the presence of a bear at a previously opened pit. Moving my safety without sound in this situation always required total concentration. I always managed it somehow — my rifle safety has never spooked a black bear.

Having spooked plenty of whitetails by inadvertently bumping my rifle on something during my 45 years of hunting, I knew from the outset that when a bear was near I'd have to make it a hard and fast rule to keep my eyes on what I was doing when guiding my rifle or bow past hazards such as tree or stand parts. All the while (I learned this the hard way), I must remain constantly aware of the position of my back — maintaining a safe distance from the noisy, rough bark of the tree behind me.

As often happens, I find I must turn my body somewhat as my sight picture slowly comes into view. Turning on a stand seat without sound also takes total concentration, especially when feet are involved. To move boots silently, slowly raise them a bit, one at a time, ease them over slowly and then lower them very cautiously. Never simply turn boots or slide them over when a bear is within short range.

Also keep track of sounds coming from inside your body. Never allow your breathing to become heavy. If your heart is tripping like a one-cylinder engine, keep your mouth shut or a bear will hear it.

5. Accept none but a perfect shot angle to the bear's heart. The animal before you is a black bear, not a deer, not a duck, not a grouse. This is no place for that *bird-in-hand, shoot and hope, empty a clip,* or *it wasn't hit bad, it'll survive* bunk. If you are not presented with a perfect shot angle today, as long as you do not alarm the bear, you will certainly get a perfect shot angle tomorrow.

When perched 9-12 feet from the ground, your rifle ready to fire or your bow at full draw, your sight(s) should be steady on one of two targets: 1) on a spot midway between the top and the bottom of the bear's chest on a vertical line directly behind the bear's near foreleg, the bear standing broadside, near foreleg extended forward, or 2) on a spot midway between the top and bottom of the bear's mid-section on a vertical line directly behind the bear's rib cage, the bear standing quartering away.

This is it...the time to make your perfect shot. You take in a deep breath, let out a little and hold. Your left arm (or rifle forearm) is braced — your aim rock-steady. You squeeze your trigger or release your arrow.

Responses of Black Bears to Hits

Heart/Lung Hits

Whether shot through the heart with an arrow or a magnum bullet, black bears of any size rarely drop in their tracks. A 225-pound boar taken by my son John flipped over backwards at the shot and was dead when it hit the ground. My son Dave's first bear — a 185-pound boar — took three quick jumps, , ran into a tree trunk and fell dead. All others barreled from the pit clearing and disappeared. All but one dropped within 35 yards. The 422-pound boar I shot last fall (bow) plunged 165 yards before dropping. All heart-shot bears went down within 20 seconds.

Three-fourths of all the heart and/or lung-shot black bears I've had a hand in taking during the past 40 years groaned (growled) three times upon going down, the third groan usually being weaker than the first two or cut short.

Other Hits

All bears but one taken by my sons, son-in-law and I were hit in the heart. One, I shot in the neck (shattering its spinal cord) at a range of 15 feet. It dropped in its tracks.

Three bears I have looked at recently were hit in the brain (shot by other hunters) They all dropped in their tracks. Their entire skulls, however, were gruesomely shattered.

One bear I inspected last fall had been shot in the neck by a bowhunter. It took three days of very skilled tracking to recover this bear.

Twice I have been asked to aid in tracking leg-shot bears. One bear was tracked 12 hours; the other three days. Sign petering out, neither was recovered.

Another I heard of recently (spring, 1990) was hit in a ham (no bone involvement). After bathing itself in the shallows of a lake some distance from where it was shot, its trail completely disappeared.

Two other bears I was asked to help recover were shot in the abdomen — one through the stomach (stomach contents identified on the bear's trail) and the other farther back (feces leaking from its wound). Neither of these fatally shot bears were found after two days of tracking.

Shot from steep shot angles by bowhunters last fall, two bears I know of were hit in scapulas (shoulder bones) and another in the spine. All ran off and none were ever seen again. At least some bears hit in the scapula with an arrow recover. The bear I took last fall had fully healed after being hit in the scapula a year or more earlier.

Another hunter I know of has shot three bears — two with a firearm and one with a bow. He has yet to recover one.

By the time two hunters I talked to last fall found their fatally crippled quarries, the bears had completely spoiled. Not even the hides could be saved.

Sad tales of crippled and lost bears are legion among hunters who fail to hit a black bear's quick-kill, heart/lung region. If such tales do not end, once and for all, bear hunting will end, once and for all.

After the Shot

It will happen fast. One second, there'll an unsuspecting black bear feeding complacently before you; the next second, it'll be gone. Unlike its approach, however, the panic-stricken bear's departure will be reckless and noisy. Likely, the bear will plunge forward in whatever direction it was facing when hit, unmindful at first of brush, trees and windfalls in its path. A fatally-wounded bear will make a lot of racket as it flees. When it can run no farther (vital tissues depleted of oxygen), it will drop to the ground, likely groan, and then quickly die.

Throughout your quarry's last desperate flight, you must keep your wits about you. It is extremely important that you follow its progress with your ears and eyes, taking note of specific landmarks along its path. When no more sounds come to your ears, dig out your compass and get an exact bearing on a distinctive landmark (a certain tree) at the spot where you last heard the bear. In the extreme excitement of the moment, it can be easy to forget all sorts of things, *but don't forget this information.* If your bullet or arrow did not make a low exit wound, this compass bearing and one landmark may be your *only* means of locating your fatally shot bear.

Now...finally...go ahead and act "human." Rejoice. Allow yourself to act like a hunter who has just succeeded in doing something quite remarkable in the annals of big game hunting. Sit back in your stand, grin, stretch, take some deep breaths and relax.

If you feel suddenly drained at this moment — your arms and legs very heavy, clumsy and shaking uncontrollably — that is "normal" under these circumstances. You're suffering the aftermath of having your body charged with enormous levels of adrenalin and blood sugar. There's nothing like bear hunting for doing that to a hunter. It'll probably take about ten minutes before you will feel capable again; able to climb to the ground in command of your body and senses. That's fine. You should remain seated in your stand for at least ten minutes at any rate. This is no time to rush off in pursuit of a bear. Let nature take its course first — in you and in the bear.

When to Begin Tracking

If you know you hit your bear in the heart/lung region, and you actually heard its death groans, there is no need to hurry. The bear isn't going anywhere. Depending somewhat on the bear's size, it is probably lying dead within 165 yards of your stand — more likely within 40 yards of your stand.

Whatever you believe at this moment, however, you should never allow yourself be absolutely certain your shot was quickly fatal. Hope it was, but **from this point on, never believe a bear is dead until the bear is down, silent, motionless, not breathing and not blinking when an eye is touched with the tip of a long sapling.** Until then, it is far wiser and far safer to accept the possibility that the bear is not only still alive, but it will be alive when you find it.

That being a distinct possibility, you must allow the fleeing bear to feel secure as soon as possible so it will lie down within the shortest possible distance from your stand. When hit, the bear probably had no idea what happened. It probably didn't connect its injury with a feared human. Even upon hearing a thunderous shot, it probably thought it was injured by another bear. If not pursued by a human soon after its initial flight, it will probably lie down within 200 yards of your bait pit. If not disturbed there, blood loss and shock will eventually take their toll, likely rooting the bear to the spot or weakening it enough to make it easy to finish. If human pursuit is evident soon after being injured, the bear will become much more alarmed than when it was initially shot. Adrenalin and blood sugar will surge through its body, not only making the bear capable of extraordinary escape efforts, but making the bear much more difficult to kill. A fully aroused black bear can absorb enormous physical injury before dying. When forced to defend itself, a fully aroused black bear might also be dangerous. Unless the bear went down within sight of your stand and you can see it hasn't moved (and hasn't made a sound) over a period of at least ten minutes, "early arousal" of a shot black bear should be avoided.

How long should you wait after the shot before taking to the trail of a bear you are not certain is dead? *At least one hour.*

Use that hour to return to camp to get rid of unneeded hunting gear, pick up a lantern and heavy-duty flashlight (if needed), enlist the aid of one or two bear tracking partners and alert your dragging crew.

Recovering a Shot Black Bear

Three Rules for Safe and Effective Tracking

1. Unless after the shot you see the bear go down and it hasn't moved or made a sound for at least ten minutes, never trail or approach an unseen, potentially live, black bear alone. Commencing no less than one hour after the shot, this is a two-man job — one keying on trail signs, the other keying on the area ahead and to either side, constantly poised to fire when the bear is sighted, if necessary.

This is not an entire, anxious-to-see-the-bear, dragging crew job. The larger the tracking group, the less likely it is that you will succeed in drawing near enough to a wounded bear to be able make an effective finishing shot. Admonish others to patiently wait in camp (or wait silently at your bait/stand site) until requested, or until some pre-arranged signal is given.

2. Move slowly and silently — absolutely no talking or whispering. Communicate via hand signals (or pencil and paper) only. Stop often and listen. Do not proceed into any area that has not first been thoroughly scanned visually. By day, use binoculars. Even in very dense cover, binoculars are very effective for spotting downed (or crippled) black bears from a safe distance.

3. From beginning (bait pit) to end (location of dead bear), generously mark the path taken by the bear. Squares of bathroom tissue impaled on high branches make wonderful trail markers, easy to spot from a distance, non-damaging to trees and biodegradable. Not only will trail markers aid in relocating a "lost trail" when sign is scant, but once the bear is found, the marked trail will probably be the surest and shortest route back to your cleared stand trail — the path you'll want to use when transporting your bear from the woods.

If you do not have an easy-to-see blood trail to follow, be sure to mark the significant landmarks you noted from your stand as the bear fled. If you cannot positively identify these landmarks from the ground, return to your stand platform and direct two partners (one watching you, the other watching for your bear) to these landmarks via silent hand signals. With your compass in hand, direct your partners (as they lay a tissue paper trail from your stand) to the exact spot where you last saw and/or heard the bear. Once these landmarks are pinpointed and marked, you can join your partner(s) to begin a more intensive — and likely more effective — search for signs and the shot bear.

Trail Signs of Wounded Bears

Blood

Whether the length of the trail to your bear is 25 yards, 165 yards, or longer, your most obvious tracking sign will be blood. If properly shot — your bullet or arrow passing through heart and lungs and making a low exit wound — profuse, external bleeding will begin within 10 yards of where the fleeing bear was hit. A spray of fine droplets of blood may be found beyond the spot where a bear stood when hit, but unlike a heart/lung shot white-tailed deer which will exude fine sprays of brightly colored blood widely to either side of its trail each time its hoofs hit the ground during flight, the trail of a rapidly fleeing, heart/lung shot black bear will typically be

Toilet tissue will keep you on the right path, day or night.

a series of large drops and elongated dollops of brightly colored blood every 1-3 yards. A black bear's dense fur, like cotton, absorbs considerable blood as it issues from the wound, causing blood to flow downward along a bear's body rather than spray outward. Wherever the fleeing bear pauses or slows down (nearing death), larger puddles of blood will be found. Drops and broad smears of blood will also become common on foliage, branches and tree trunks brushed by the fleeing bear — mostly on the side of the exit wound. The quantity of blood will gradually increase or remain steady. Such a blood trail will usually lead quickly to a very dead bear.

Keep in mind a black bear can travel 30+mph, meaning one could theoretically cover 293+ yards in 20 seconds. However, I have never personally known a heart-shot black bear to travel farther than 165 yards.

If your bullet or arrow passed through heart and lungs but does not make an exit wound, little or no blood sign is likely to be found until very near the place where the bear went down. It takes considerable hemorrhaging inside before significant blood can fill the chest to the height of the wound and make its way through the fat and hair about a high entry wound. By the time significant bleeding begins, the bear may already be dead.

A trail that begins with profuse bleeding but wanes — spots of blood becoming fewer, smaller and/or farther apart — means the bear was not hit in the heart/lung region.

If the bear (not immediately pursued) laid down within 100-200 yards — its bed identified via flattened vegetation and pooled blood — the bear was *seriously* wounded; probably *fatally* wounded.

Keeping in mind the height of blood smears noted along the bear's escape trail and the direction a wounded bear will face when lying down (toward its back trail), the position of blood evident within or about the area of flattened vegetation will reveal the location of the bear's wound(s). By placing yourself in the same general position in relationship to the bear's bed as at the time of the shot (the bear's head right or left), you should be able to determine from the location of the blood in the bed where (what part of it's anatomy) the bear was hit.

If hit anywhere within its abdominal cavity (from rib cage back), the bear will certainly die; probably within six hours if its liver or kidneys were damaged; more slowly (perhaps taking 1-3 days or longer) if its stomach, intestines and/or urinary bladder were damaged.

If the blood trail begins quickly enough, bleeding profuse at first, but then blood gradually ebbs, perhaps abating completely within 100-300 yards (the bear not lying down within that distance), it is likely the bear was hit in a leg or ham with no bone damage, a non-vital area of its neck or a superficial part of its body. Considerable skill and determination will be required to recover the bear.

Hair

Scattered black bear hairs alone at the shot site reveal the bear was hit, but they cannot reveal how seriously. Long black hairs probably mean it was hit in the torso somewhere; short, wiry black hairs, in a lower limb. When trailing a bear that otherwise provided no evidence of being injured, black hairs found clinging to branches along a bear's escape route do not necessarily mean a hit was registered.

White hairs at the shot site indicate the the bullet or arrow pierced the bear's brisket, white blazes not uncommon high on the chests (beneath their necks) of black bears. If shot with an arrow while quartering away, white hairs generally mean the heart was missed but the near lung was damaged, a wound which may or may not be quickly fatal on a medium-to-large bruin. If white hairs are found after a shot was taken head-on, using a high-powered rifle caliber such as a 175-grain, 7mm Magnum (a shot angle to be avoided when using a bow), the trail to the bear will likely be very short, the heart and/or large blood vessels at the top of the heart almost assuredly damaged. It takes plenty of foot-pounds energy, however, to penetrate deeply enough into a black bear from this angle. With lesser calibers, lung damage is certain, but not necessarily with abruptly fatal effect.

Short tan hairs at the shot site indicate the bear was hit in the muzzle. A bear hit in the muzzle that does not immediately fall will be most difficult to recover, and if not recovered, it may live a considerable time before dying from its wound or starving to death, unable to consume foods.

Bone

Bone fragments may be found at the shot site or along the bear's escape route. Rib bone fragments — relatively thin with flat surfaces— usually reveal a hit that will be quickly fatal (heart/lung hit). Bone fragments that are thick and rounded usually mean the bear was hit in a limb. Such a fragment may come from a lower shoulder bone. Hit in the lower shoulder by a bullet — the bear standing broadside.— the wound will probably be quickly fatal; hit there with an arrow, the wound will likely be very slowly fatal.

Other Bodily Substances

Bloody, undigested or partially digested bits of recognizable bear foods mean the bear was hit in the stomach. Bloody feces (droppings) and/or urine mean it was hit far back in the abdomen. Though there are major blood vessels in the abdomen that when hit can cause massive bleeding and a quickly fatal effect (descending aorta and ascending vena cava), stomach or intestinal contents generally mean a long and arduous trail lies before the hunter, a live bear at the end.

Other Trail Signs

Heart or lung-shot, a black bear will flee with little regard for lesser obstacles in its path. Though not always obvious, off-trail foliage and branches along its escape route will be bent (in the direction taken by the bear), ripped, trampled and/or broken. If an established deer trail is handy, a wounded bear will likely use it, meaning, damaged vegetation and branches are not *always* evident.

Especially where the ground is wet or soft, a fleeing bear's paw prints will reveal haste, tracks appearing ragged, freshly turned leaves, twigs and fresh soil or mud scattered fore and aft.

When on the bloodless trail of a wounded bear (no exit wound), it is important to mark the locations of less obvious signs (preferably with white tissue paper). Indistinct signs will soon lose their appearance of "freshness" and human passage can easily destroy them. Each indistinct sign by itself my be only suggestive of of a fleeing bear, but when each is marked, many will line up to form an obvious trail.

200-Plus-Yard Trails

A wounded black bear that travels more than 200 yards without lying down was obviously not hit in the heart. For that matter, it was probably not hit in a lung either, meaning, it will be a tough bear to recover.

Whatever the case, it is a hunter's obligation to make every attempt to secure a speedy and humane end to the suffering of a wounded black bear. Not only is it ethically and morally wrong to shirk such a duty, but if you do, you may even indirectly endanger the lives of innocent humans that may accidently stumble upon your wounded bear. Upon making the decision to hunt black bears, those who expect you to return to home or job should be made aware of the fact that things may not go according to plan. You might find it necessary to spend an extra day or two afield in order to properly finish your bear.

Lost Trail

Under the best of circumstances, a wounded bear's trail is easily lost. After the shot, the bear may travel a considerable distance before external bleeding begins. It may flee through impregnable cover, water and/or over treacherous terrain where detours are necessary. The bear may pause to lick its wound, causing the trail to suddenly disappear. Loose fat beneath the bear's hide may temporarily plug the wound. The bear may double back on its trail and then turn off at an unexpected place. Falling rain may wash away sign in unprotected areas. Darkness may add to the burden.. There are lots of reasons for temporarily losing the trail.

When the trail is suddenly lost, return to the last identified sign, it's location marked by a square of white tissue paper impaled on an high overhanging branch. Using the line of tissue papers behind you as a guide, move five yards to one side, circle through a 180-degree arc (half-circle) ahead — searching carefully for signs as you go — until at a right angle on the opposite side of the end of the trail. Now move out another five yards and begin another circling movement, continuing in this manner through ever widening arcs until the bear's trail is once again discovered.

If upon searching through ten of such arcs (now 50 yards from the end of the trail), the bear's escape route is not yet discovered, suspect one of three possibilities: 1) the bear quit bleeding for one reason or another, 2) it turned sharply away or back from its line of flight or 3) it is lying dead where not easily spotted near the end of the trail. Mortally wounded black bears not uncommonly make a J-like movement to one side or the other shortly before death. Go back, then, to the last sign and begin making ever-widening, "full circles" about this point until the bear or its trail is discovered. If necessary, course out to 100 yards from the end of the trail.

When All Else Fails

No bear sign within 100 yards? No blood, no tracks, no freshly broken branches or no flattened vegetation? Now what? *Do it again*, only this time occasionally mark your progress with squares of tissue paper to make sure you do not miss an area greater than five yards in width. If you still fail to find a trail or a dead bear, extend your search out to 150 yards. Failing out to 150 yards from your last sign, there is little more you can do, except, perhaps, continue out to 200 yards. If a search of this magnitude does not turn up something, assume the bear was not as seriously wounded as you thought, it quit bleeding and has left the area.

Night Tracking

Trailing a bruin in the dark is not an uncommon necessity in black bear hunting. There are two reasons: 1) black bears are often shot shortly before sunset and 2) dead black bears — undressed — spoil very quickly. The trouble is, it is illegal to carry a firearm or bow in the woods after sunset. Unless I am absolutely certain I have hit a bear perfectly (I shot it through the heart), I saw it fall and thereafter it did not move or make a sound and/or I heard its death groans, I would not attempt the eerie task of trailing and approaching a medium-to-large, wounded black bear in the dark without the protection of a loaded weapon. It's risky enough by daylight.

When certain my bear is dead, I'll return to camp, trade hunting gear for tracking and field dressing equipment — including a strong, 6-volt flashlight and a double-mantel Coleman lantern — enlist the aid of one or two hunting partners for tracking and get my dragging crew ready.

Bear blood is especially easy to spot in the glow of a Coleman lantern — appearing almost fluorescent — making night tracking relatively easy. If, however, the blood signs typical of a heart/lung shot bear are not evident, rather than take the chance of spoiling the appearance of the trail via human passage, or rather than taking the chance of stumbling upon a live, wounded bear, while unarmed, break off the search and wait until first light in the morning.

With one of my partners intently following a blood trail, glowing lantern in hand, I like to keep to one side, using my 6-volt lantern to study black objects ahead. A gas lantern does not have enough range to suit me, especially since it must often be held low while tracking. If we were to unwittingly approach a wounded bear that was still alive, I want as wide a margin of safety as possible. My 6-volt flashlight, then, is one of those that casts a beam up to twelve miles.

Approaching a Downed Black Bear

Upon spotting a bear-like object on the ground ahead, a silent council is held, each of us giving whatever it is a thorough once-over with the light. If the bear is lying facing its back trail, it will be relatively easy to identify from a distance. In the beam of a flashlight, its eyes will glow silvery, even when dead, and its tawny muzzle will be evident. Once satisfied it is indeed a bear, and it seems dead, from a distance of at least 20 yards I'll sling a rock or dead branch beyond it, watching for a reaction. Seeing none, I'll then creep silently forward — alone — circling widely toward the bear's rear or backside.

Black bears almost always die lying on one side or the other. I would be suspicious of a bear lying square on its stomach, paws and head extended forward; doubly suspicious if its eyes were closed. Eyes remain open when black bears die. At night, if things didn't look "right," I'd retreat with all caution and check the bear again an hour later.

After circling to its rear or backside, from a distance of at least 10 yards, I'll spend about a minute or so watching the bear's rib cage — making certain the bear isn't breathing. Upon seeing no breathing motions, I'll swing my light to the bear's eyes, watching for the least flicker. Signs of life absent, I'll then reach for a long, slender stick and stealthily stalk nearer, keeping to the bear's backside. In this location, it would be difficult for a bear to strike in my direction with claw or fang. Leaning out, my light on the bear's easiest-to-reach eye, I'll gently touch the pupil with the end of my stick. If the eye does not blink — the last reflex to go — the bear is truly dead.

When approaching a downed bear during daylight hours, legally armed, use no less caution. Keep your eyes on the bear, your weapon ready to fire. Move forward in the above prescribed manner, first watching for breathing motions and then checking for an eye reflex before touching the bear.

Finishing Shots — Downed Bears

Paul Fox, my Yukon grizzly bear guide, always directed his hunters to take a finishing shot. "Shoot it in the neck whether it shows any signs of life or not," he'd say, "just to be sure." Whether hunting dangerous grizzlies or docile black bears, I'm not so sure a neck shot is the ultimate finishing shot. If you can be sure of hitting a black bear's slender neck vertebrae (spinal bones), a neck shot will immediately anchor a bear for good. Having found spent bullets under fully-healed hides on the necks of at least two black bears and one grizzly, however, it is obvious to me that the spine is easy to miss in a broad-necked bear, especially when the hunter is excited (which is guaranteed).

Knowing a bone fide heart shot will stop a black bear within 10-20 seconds, I'd go for the heart if I ever had a reason to take a finishing shot.

I do not think it's necessary to shoot a black bear a second time unless there is reason to believe the bear is still alive, however. Unnecessary second shots have a habit of ruining choice cuts of meat and/or trophies.

Finishing Shots — Moving Bears

Finishing a wounded black bear that is still alive, able to travel and in command if its senses is a considerable challenge. Unless winds are strong or moderate-to-heavy rain is falling, it can be very difficult to stalk near enough for a finishing shot, especially within the heavy, difficult-to-penetrate, noisy cover (wooded swamp) a wounded black bear will likely lead the hunter. Enormous stealth — two-men silently stalking — is an essential prerequisite; also courage and reliable shooting instincts. When the bear is at last discovered, fueled by surging adrenalin, it will probably be seen plunging away through dense cover — a fleeting target at best. If I was a trophy-hunting bowhunter caught in this situation, I guess I'd forget about "Pope and Young" and start thinking "Boone and Crockett." For the bear's sake and mine, I'd forsake my bow and load up Big Boomer (my Ruger 7mm Magnum) for this job.

Particularly if the wounded black bear is large, this is the circumstance in which you should gird yourself for the possibility of danger. It is altogether likely a wounded black bear will do everything in its power to keep away from you, but never count on it. Always proceed as if you are going to have to fire at an approaching bear within very short range.

I guess if I was ever charged by a black bear, I guess I wouldn't worry much about ruining a trophy skull. I'd aim at the oncoming bear's head, an eye or the mouth my intended target. Between a black bear's eyes, the skull is thick and angled almost straight back. Hit between the eyes from ground level, a bullet might actually ricochet upward, but it would certainly stun the bear, probably dropping it in its tracks. Hit in an eye, a bullet would easily range back into the bear's brain, perhaps exploding the brain cavity, but immediately dropping the bear. At ground level, a bullet entering an approaching black bear's mouth would enter the most vital of brain tissues or the bear's spine beneath its skull, in either case instantly dropping the bear. If I had a chance for a heart shot, I'd take it, but upon meeting a feisty bruin head-on at close quarters, I wouldn't mess around trying for a perfect shot. I'd aim at quick-kill target areas as best I could, and I wouldn't quit firing until the bear was down for keeps.

The Almost Mythical Charge

Though probably a one-in-a-million event, an unstoppable charge by an enraged black bear is every hunter's worst nightmare. It's the underlying cause of poor shooting; the dread that contributes most to making black bear hunting the thrilling adventure it is. Though *extremely* unlikely, a few unfortunate hunters have experienced such a charge, and likely a few more will experience such charges in the future.

If you were to suddenly find yourself in this situation — being unable to protect yourself, charged and mauled by a black bear — the recommended course of action is to immediately "play dead." Drop to the ground, curl into a fetal position, legs drawn up to protect your abdomen and hands and arms wrapped about your head and neck. If the bear thinks you're dead, it will soon become satisfied that it has accomplished what it set out to do, and it will leave. Black bears do not eat humans, so don't worry about that. Regardless of any injuries you may suffer, don't move or make a sound unless absolutely necessary for at least fifteen minutes after your attacker has departed. If near, your movements or sounds may trigger another attack. After fifteen minutes have passed, attend to your wounds and then head for help or stay put until help arrives. When bear hunting, make it a "standard procedure" in your group that someone will head to your stand if you do not show up in camp within an hour or so after dark.

There is a better alternative, of course — shoot 'em properly to start with. Doing that, you'll never have to make a finishing shot, you'll never have to follow a live, wounded bear in a cedar swamp and you'll never have to face a charging black bear.

Kill Site Photos

Okay Dan'l, you can stop holding your breath. It's all over. Go ahead and cheer if you have a mind too. You deserve to be elated. You did a good job. You've accomplished something few hunters have accomplished. And like all bear hunters before you, not only did you harvest a much-revered black bear, but you obviously conquered something pretty tough to conquer inside. It's all something to be especially proud of.

Boy, look at that bear. What a beauty, hey? Look at the size of that neck. And those claws. Awesome. Is that fur ever thick and silky. Wow, he's heavy.

Hey, where's the camera?

Bear country photographs are the best. A picture of you standing by a bear hanging from garage rafters just doesn't do it. Photos of you (still somewhat dazed) and your bear (not yet field dressed) in the wilds where it lived carry enormous impact. You'll value such photos the rest of your life. In fact, succeeding generations of your family will consider such photos to be very precious — *Great-grandpa with the bear he got back in 1990. Wow, was he ever something!*

Do it right. Dig out some paper toweling and wipe all visible blood from the bear. Tuck its tongue back into its mouth. Kneel beside it, holding the bear's head. Don't sit on the bear and don't position yourself five feet behind the bear to make it look larger than it really is. Don't make photos that lie. You won't fool anyone. Be proud, but don't act like a conquering hero; an egomaniac. Handle your bear in a manner that reflects your respect for this once mighty creature. Do it right and you'll ever be proud to show others your photos. Taken in good taste, others will also enjoy looking at your photos.

Chapter 7

Black Bear Harvest

The black bear you have just taken will be every bit as much trouble as a mink covered carton containing 250-500 pounds of 100-degree milk. Now you must quickly remove innards capable of seriously contaminating bear meat, move a carcass weighing 250-500 pounds from the woods without damaging its valuable pelt, and then get the carcass and pelt cooled before they spoil. Under the same conditions, a 250-500 pound bear will sour about as quickly a carton containing 250-500 pounds of 100-degree milk. When the air temperature is about 40°F., a bear carcass (field dressed) and its pelt will begin to spoil in about 12 hours; when 50°F., in about 6 hours; when 60°F., in about 3 hours. Upon taking a bear, then, time is of the essence.

Field Dressing

Before you kneel to begin field dressing your bear, remember what your bear has been eating — that rotten-smelling, fly and maggot-infested stuff in your bait pit. Would you eat a steak that has been dipped in the stuff found in your bait pit? Would you get sick if you did? Well, encased within your bear's stomach and intestines is plenty of undigested, partially digested and fully digested stuff from your bait pit. If any of it escapes into the abdominal cavity as you field dress your bear, you will be eating bear steaks that have been dipped in stuff from in your bait pit (something to think about, too, when taking aim at a bear — don't hit stomach or intestines).

Considering this sobering thought, it should be obvious field dressing a black bear demands skill and knowledge; considerably more than is demonstrated by the average whitetail hunter. Whitetails being herbivores, hunters can get away with improper field dressing to a degree, but not bear hunters. It must be done exactly right.

Compared to a white-tailed deer, the contents of a black bear's chest and abdominal cavities are relatively small. Bear lungs are considerably smaller than those of whitetails and they have a much smaller stomach (not being four-chambered like a whitetail). The viscera of a whitetail accounts for 22-23% of its total body weight; that of a black bear, about 10-15% of its total weight (less in larger bears).

Field dressing accomplishes three important functions: 1) it reduces the weight of a bear, making its transport easier, 2) it removes substances potentially ruinous to the wholesomeness of the meat and 3) it greatly enhances cooling of the carcass, vital to both the meat and the pelt.

All you need for field dressing a black bear is a *sharp* knife, a short length of stout cord, a gallon-sized plastic bag (optional) and some paper towelling (to wipe your hands and arms when you're done). If it's dark, you'll also need light — both your lantern and your flashlight will be needed, plus someone to hold and move them about.

If your knife isn't sharp, you're going to do plenty of cussin' when cutting through tough bear hide. Bear hide comes close to moose hide for toughness, and like moose hide, it'll dull a poor knife in a hurry. Your knife's blade should be no longer than 2-1/2 - 4 inches in length. A short blade is safer, it works better in small places (such as in the chest cavity) and it puts your hand closer to your work, giving you greater control. Imagine a surgeon trying to do his work using one of those monstrous, Bowie-type knives carried by so many hunters these days.

The ten steps to properly field dressing a black bear are as follows:

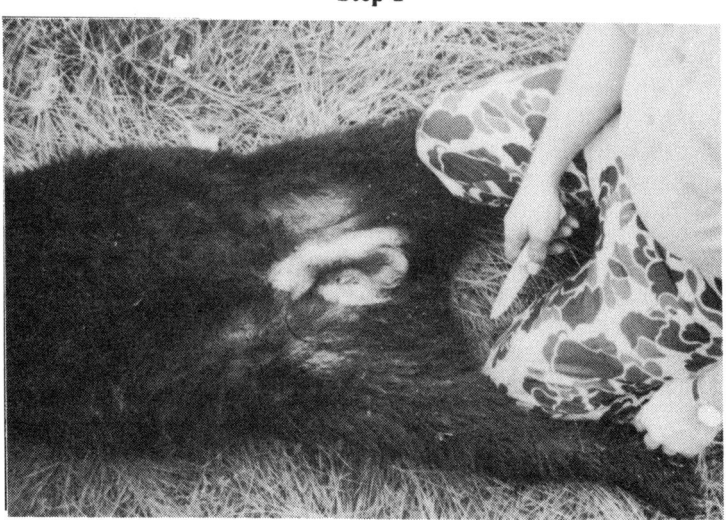

Step 1

Step 1a

Roll the bear onto its back. With hind legs spread (tied to adjacent trees or held by hunting partners), cut through the hide around the bear's penis and testicles (or vulva on sow), separating the penis and testicles from underlying body tissues down to the pelvic canal from which the shaft of the penis emerges. Do not sever the penis or testicles from the carcass (avoid cutting through a sow's vagina as the vulva is separated from underlying tissues).

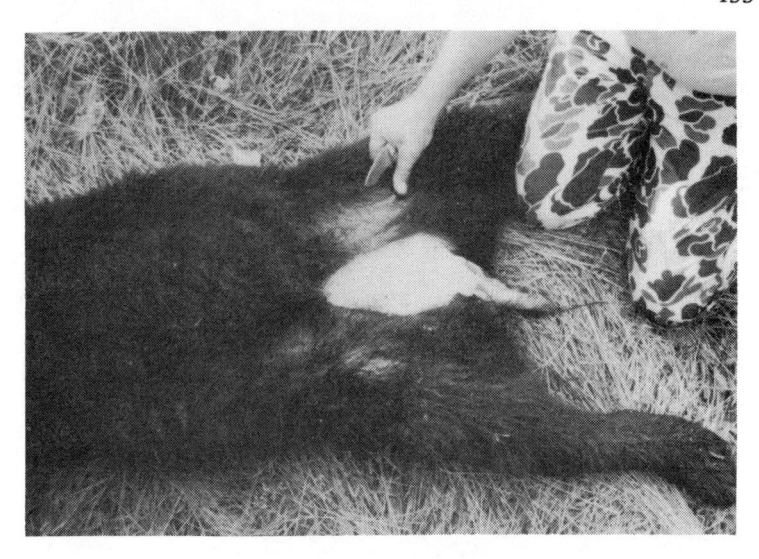

Step1b

Step 2

Continuing the cuts made through the hide on either side of the penis and testicles (or vulva), cut through the hide completely around the bear's anus. Carefully separate the anus, rectum and penis shaft from surrounding tissues about four inches into the bony pelvic canal. Where it wraps around the pubic bone, you'll find the penis shaft is attached by a thick,

Step 2

strong tendon. Using your knife, slice through this tendon close to the bone. Once severed, much of the connective tissue about that portion of the penis that passes through the bony pelvic canal and much of that about the rectum can be separated by inserting a finger, curling it alongside the pelvic bones and pulling outward. Connective tissues that will not separate via this technique should be carefully severed with the tip of your knife blade.

Step 3

Now grasp the separated base of the penis (or vagina) and rectum firmly in your left hand and stretch them outward from the pelvic canal.

Step 4

Steps 3 and 4

Firmly wrap a stout cord twice about the out-stretched base of the penis (or vagina) and rectum and tie the ends tightly with a square knot. Now urine and feces cannot escape from from the bear's urinary bladder or rectum during the rest of the field dressing process.

Step 5

With the blade of your knife held upright, extend the cut made in the pelvic area up the center of the bear's abdomen to the the base of the breastbone (sternum), slicing upward through the hide only. Spreading the hide as you go, next carefully slice down through the fatty tissue overlying the smooth, white peritoneum (the sack that contains the bowels).

Step 5a

Using the tip of your knife, carefully make a small incision through the peritoneum just forward of the bear's pubic bone. Kneeling on one side of the bear and facing its tail end, insert two fingers of your left hand into the incision, curl them back at the second knuckle and lift the peritoneum from the underlying bowels. Insert the tip of your knife, blade up, be-

Step 5b

Step 5c

tween your fingers, being careful to avoid piercing intestines. Cut carefully toward the breastbone as your left fingers slide along on either side of the blade, lifting the peritoneum away from the bowels as you continue. Now the abdominal cavity is open.

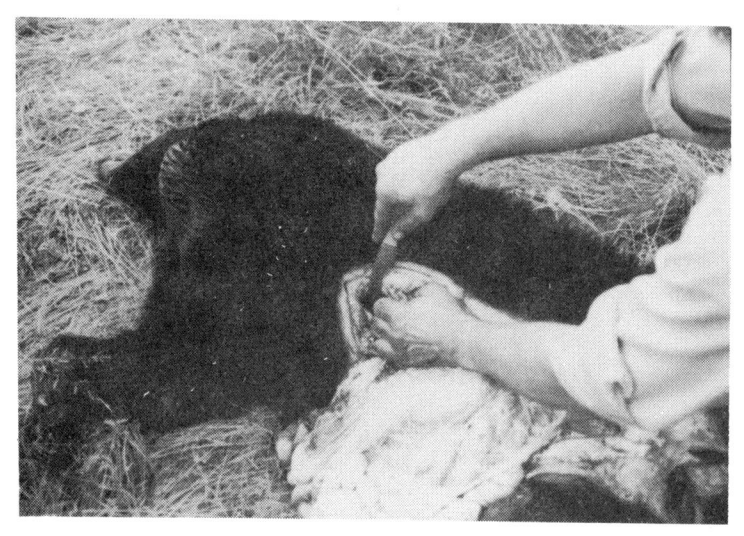

Step 6

Step 6

Spread open the abdominal incision. Reach in and gently part the bear's liver from tissues below the lower end of the breastbone to expose the bear's diaphragm — a thin layer of muscle that separates the chest cavity from the abdominal cavity. This muscle must be severed from the body cavity completely around the inner surfaces of the lowest ribs on both sides, breastbone to backbone. In a fat bear, this can be difficult to accomplish. Not uncommonly, the bear must be rolled a bit bit to one side and then the other in order to move the liver and stomach enough to see the diaphragm deep on either side. If the entire diaphragm cannot be cut without being in danger of cutting open the stomach of the bear, leave the lower portion of the diaphragm (near the spine) intact at this point, finishing it up after the bear's lungs and heart are pulled from the chest cavity (making the lower diaphragm easier to see and reach).

Step 7

You should now be able to see (somewhat) into the chest cavity. If you shot your bear properly, the bear's lungs will be collapsed and the chest cavity will be half full of blood. Roll up your sleeves and reach forward (toward the neck) into the chest cavity with both hands, knife in one.

Step 7a

Caution: if you shot your bear with an arrow and the arrow did not pass entirely through the chest cavity, be sure to remove it before reaching blindly into the chest cavity. A broadhead can do a nasty job on your hands. Use your free hand to locate and grasp the bundle of tubes emerg-

Step 7b

ing into the front part of the chest cavity from the bear's neck. One tube in that bundle is easy to identify via feel. It will feel like a metal conduit — firm with projecting rings. That's the bear's trachea or windpipe. On both sides and beneath the trachea, you'll feel other tubes — soft in your grasp. The big one beneath the trachea is the esophagus — the tube connecting from the bear's mouth to its stomach. The smaller tubes are major blood vessels coursing to and from the bear's head and neck. Firmly grasp this entire bundle of tubes in one hand, pulling back on it a bit as you carefully ease your knife (blade down and at a right angle to the spine) to a point halfway between your hand holding the bundle of tubes and the base of the neck. Now, using short strokes, cut down through the bundle of tubes until it is fully severed. Don't let go at this point. Ease your knife hand out and then pull the severed bundle of tubes from the chest. Emerging from the chest cavity — attached to those tubes — will be the bear's heart and lungs. Just like that, the bear's chest cavity will be empty, except for free blood.

Step 8

Now roll the bear carcass to one side. By partially rolling loose viscera from the abdominal cavity and having a partner lift up the top edge of the abdominal incision, you should be able to see and cut through (along the ribs) any of the diaphragm you couldn't get at before. You'll probably have to roll the bear to the other side to finish the diaphragm cut. Once the diaphragm is completely free, the bear's stomach and intestines will seem more inclined to emerge from the abdominal cavity, but not

Step 8

fully — they're still attached to something somewhere. What they're attached to is a curtain of thin tissue (omentum) which is attached to the spine in the forward half the the abdominal cavity. With the stomach and intestines partially rolled from the abdominal cavity (carcass on one side), if you can't see this spinal attachment, you should nonetheless easily locate with your hands. Carefully reach in over the stomach and liver with both hands, knife in one hand, the other hand pressing tissues aside to expose the omentum where its attaches at the spine. Carefully cut through these tissues where they attach to the (lumpy) spine. As you do this, you'll note the stomach and intestines are falling free from the inner carcass. Be careful not to cut into the tenderloins (long, thin muscle bundles) located on either side of the spine. Once this 8-12 inch-long section of omentum is severed, the entire mass of viscera will roll free from the chest and abdominal cavities, except the intestine and other tubes that course back toward the anus through the inner end of the bony pelvic girdle between the bear's hind legs.

Step 9

With most of the viscera removed — intestine and other tubes intact where they enter the pelvic canal inside, roll the bear carcass to its back so you can see what you're going to do next. You don't want to goof up here. Using fingers, and your knife when you have to, carefully separate the tissues surrounding the intestine and other tubes from the inner end of the bony pelvic canal. Usually about 4 inches in is enough, but you might soon find it necessary to separate pelvic tissues from the bony pelvis an-

Step 9a

other inch or two at both ends of the canal. Now, firmly grasp the bowel and other tissues right next to where they enter the inner end of the pelvic canal. Slowly and firmly pull these tissues toward the head end of the carcass. The tied rectum and penis shaft (or vagina) should soon begin sliding into and through the pelvic canal. If they do not, stop and carefully separate surrounding tissues more deeply at both ends of the pelvic canal.

Step 9b

Whatever you do, do not cut into the intestine or the urethra (thin tube from bladder to external penis or vulva). Once the tied rectum and penis shaft (or vulva) slides into and entirely through the pelvic canal, the entire visceral mass can be rolled free from the carcass.

Step 10

Now roll the bear carcass back-side-up, legs spread to both sides, head end slanted uphill if possible, to allow the blood inside the carcass to drain from the abdominal incision.

If the bear's heart was not hit and you like venison heart meat (high in cholesterol), you'll also enjoy bear heart meat. You'll find it inside a rough-textured sack (pericardium) between the bear's collapsed lungs. Cut an opening in one side of this sack, cut the heart free from the sack and blood vessels attached to the top of the heart, squeeze the heart to remove clotted blood and drop the heart into a plastic bag for transport to camp.

Don't take black bear liver. As you can see, a black bear's liver is strange in appearance — pale and/or yellow. It is so loaded with vitamin B that it can be toxic. Leave it for the birds and other wild creatures.

Step 10

Okay, wipe your hands and arms and retrieve your knife. This job is done.

Transporting Your Bear to Camp

A Bear Too Big to Handle

Last fall, I shot a 422-pound bear on the evening of the third day of my hunt, some hours, unfortunately, after most of the members of my pre-arranged dragging crew had to head home. Upon completing field dressing chores, my daughter, Peggy (anxious to get home to relieve a babysitter), son-in-law, Kevin, and I realized we (I) had a big problem. There was no way the three of us were going to be able to drag this bear 3/5ths of a mile through alder swamp and forest to the nearest road. We could hardly turn the bear over for field dressing. This job was going to require some special equipment.

Fortunately, the temperature was in the mid-40s. I decided it would be safe to leave the bear in the woods overnight while I scrambled to procure help. The carcass could not be left on the ground, however. The part resting against the ground would surely spoil overnight. Using screw-in tree steps, plenty of stout rope and my hand winch, we raised the bear carcass up into an adjacent birch tree via ropes tied firmly about the bears lower hind legs. I did not want to tie a rope about the bear's neck for fear of ruining the condition of the luxuriant fur there.

To enhance cooling, I propped the abdominal incision open with a pair of 10-inch long sticks sharpened at the ends (to prevent slipping). Wolves being prevalent in the area, I hung a sweaty shirt from the bear's outstretched front legs to keep them away.

Shortly after daybreak the next morning, a local logger named Wayne Revell and a neighbor drove a pair of chained-together ATVs (one a 4WD), followed by a large sled, right to my bear, the trail across a spruce bog cleared a bit here and there with my chainsaw. We dropped the bear squarely on the sled. Within 30 minutes we were shoving and pulling the bear carcass into the back of my pickup for its 1-1/2 hour trip to the butcher.

Did I make it in time? It was close. Happily, I ended up with 276 pounds of boned bear meat, equal in flavor to any I have ever tasted in all my years of bear hunting.

Dragging

Black bears are never easy to drag. They spread out on the ground, cutting a wide swath, making them seem twice as heavy as they really are. Moreover, as the carcass is dragged over the ground, the fur — one of the most valued parts of a bear carcass — is easy damaged and the meat is easily contaminated. To make dragging easier (providing a slippery surface) and to protect the fur and meat, we routinely roll the carcass up in a tough (reinforced), plastic tarp — tying the ends securely with ropes,

Tootsie Roll fashion. Then we roll the front end of the carcass onto one of our bait hauling sleds and tie it down in several places.

As my gang and I have learned over the years, a 30-foot length of 1/2 or 3/4-inch Manila rope makes an ideal bear dragging rope. One end is fastened to the sled's lead rope and the rope around the lead end of the Tootsie Roll tarp. A wide loop (10 feet of rope) is tied at the other end, several knots or smaller (hand-sized) loops tied in between.

The wide loop harness at the lead end is used by the strongest member of the dragging crew (usually my son, Dave). The hunter steps into this loop, raises the lead end up and back behind his neck with sides of the loop passing back under his armpits. Leaning forward and driving with the legs — arms free to part branches and handle a flashlight — this is a most comfortable and effective harness for dragging heavy loads across the ground.

The rest of the crew lines up behind the lead man on one side of the rope, grabbing knots or loops (non-slip handholds) at wide enough intervals to keep from tripping over one another. Hauling a bear single file in this manner, a large dragging crew can very efficiently worm its way along narrow, winding trails. When hauling two abreast, it seems someone is always tripping, falling, tearing clothing or getting poked in an eye, especially when dragging a bear in the dark.

If you have a large bear, rough or steep terrain, a long distance and/or warm temperatures facing you, it's not a bad idea to pack some liquid refreshments to keep your draggin' crew happy.

Field and Camp Care of a Bear Carcass

Once your bear's in camp, give it a little TLC. To start the vital cooling process, immediately unwrap the carcass from the heat-retaining plastic dragging tarp. Then, if it is cool enough and you are not planning to take it immediately to a registration station and a walk-in cooler (meat processor), as soon as possible, hang the carcass off the ground, propping the abdominal incision wide open with sharp-ended sticks. If a heavy tree branch or meat rack is not handy, if you lack adequate muscle power or don't have a winch to raise a bear from the ground, hang the carcass from a sturdy tripod (three poles tied together at one end). With the ends of the poles splayed widely, tie the lower ends (ankles?) of the bear's hind legs to the center with as short a rope as possible (lifting the rump end of the carcass). Raise the bear by sliding the outer ends of the poles toward the bear, one-by-one. Using a tripod, one or two men can easily raise a hefty bear without special equipment. A tripod can also be handy for loading a heavy bear into a vehicle.

Also, whether you plan to immediately transport your bear to a cooler or not, as soon as you get to camp (or your vehicle), take the time to make sure the inside of the carcass is clean and free of blood. Wipe it thoroughly with paper towels. Also make sure the pelvic canal is completely open. Free air passage through this opening is important to preserving the wholesomeness of meat in the bear's rump and hind quarters — the area where a bear's heat-retaining fat is the thickest.

If flies, wasps and other insects are after your bear carcass, cover it with cheese cloth or mosquito netting. Don't spray it with insect repellant.

Emergency Measures for Saving Bear Hide and Meat

Quickly hang the carcass, body cavity propped open to enhance cooling.

If faced with the prospect of not being able to get your bear carcass to a cooler in time to prevent spoilage, don't give up. Even when tissues along the abdominal incision are starting to turn bluish-green and the carcass isn't smelling so great, you might yet be able to save it.

Wherever the bear is located (in the woods or camp), the first thing to do — after sending someone to town to get plenty of ice (and ice chests, if needed) — is place the carcass on a clean tarp and skin it, leaving the head and paws intact (attached to the hide). After skinning, trim from the carcass and hide all the fat you can, discarding it; also, tainted meat. Then, using a sharp knife and bone saw (or sharp axe), cut the carcass into chunks that will fit into ice chests. Once you have the hide and meat on ice, you can relax a bit. If the ice lasts, your meat will probably be safe for another 3-6 hours.

If you anticipate this sort of a problem, take plenty of ice chests — loaded with block ice — when heading to bear camp. To make ice last longer, add a 4-5 pound brick of dry ice to each cooler, sealing the chests with duct tape. If you keep your coolers sealed and in the shade, the added dry ice will make regular block ice will last up to a week.

If you're really up a tree — no ice — wrap each part of your skinned and cut-up bear in waterproof plastic bags (no air) and drop them into a shady spot in a cool stream or lake Depending on how cool the water is, this will give you a little breathing room, but not much.

Your bear pelt can be preserved with salt. The only trouble is, if salt is your only alternative, you're going to have to skin out the bear's head and paws — a risky proposition if you don't know what you're doing and if you're planning to have the head mounted (whether for a bear rug, wall mount or full mount). The tough parts are ears (preserving cartilage), eyes (saving skin well back into the sockets), nose (preserving skin well back into the nostrils), lips (preserving skin well onto the tissues surrounding teeth and then splitting the lips) and toes (saving the toe pads). Upon doing all this, the hide must be scraped free of flesh and fat before salting. Apply plenty of uniodized salt, rubbing it thoroughly into all parts of the hide. Spread (fur side down) or hang it it in a shady, airy place to dry. Blot or pour off any liquids that gather on the hide, adding more salt to wet spots. Drying will take several days. Once dry, the hide will hold up for a considerable time. Keep it dry, well aired and free from insects and wild creatures that eat hides and/or love salt.

Transporting Your Bear in a Vehicle

Everything you've done to make sure your bear will arrive fresh at a meat processing plant, and taxidermist, can be easily ruined during your trip home. Especially on a sunny day, never transport a bear carcass in a tightly enclosed space. The worse thing you could do is cover it with a tarp and then close it up in your car trunk. Regardless of air temperatures outside, latent heat in the carcass, plus heat provided by the sun shining on an unventilated space, can not only ruin bear meat within a couple of hours, but cause bear hair to pull loose in handfuls (slippage) the next time the carcass is handled. Wherever you put the carcass, give it plenty of ventilation. If you must put it in a trunk, leave the trunk lid open; in a pickup box with a topper, open all the windows.

If you have a long trip ahead of you, it would be wise to have your bear skinned and processed by a butcher in the area where you hunt, picking up frozen meat and the hide at a later date. Doing this will insure your meat and hide will be of highest quality.

Skinning

Because daytime temperatures are not often favorable for chilling and storing bear meat during the usual dates of black bear hunting seasons, unless you have your own walk-in cooler, it is unlikely that you will ever find it convenient to skin and butcher your own bear. Nonetheless, it is not uncommon for a butcher to ask, "How do you want your bear skinned?" This usually means the butcher is not sure how to do it, taxidermy in mind. If for no other reason, you should know how it should be done.

Though the hide comes easy from a bear carcass, the job of skinning a bear is not easy for three reasons: 1) the entire hide (rather than merely antlers as on a whitetail) is normally the trophy part of a black bear, meaning, great care must be exercised throughout the skinning process, 2) the head and paws must remain a part of the hide and 3) soft (liquified if it's warm) and slippery bear fat will eventually cover everything within five feet of the hide, including the skinner(s).

The manner in which you skin a bear depends a great deal on what you plan to have a taxidermist do with your hide — make a bear rug (most common), make a shoulder (wall) mount or make a full body mount (becoming more common).

Whatever you have in mind, begin by placing the carcass on its back on a large, clean, plastic tarp spread on the floor or hang the carcass via a stout rope (or large meat hook) run through and around the front of exposed pelvic girdle. An intact boney pelvis will easily support the heaviest bear. The carcass will look strange with its hind legs draped downward, but when skinning, don't hang the bear by its legs or neck.

For skinning, you won't need much in the way of tools — a short-bladed knife with plenty of curve near the tip and a bone saw. A hack saw with a coarse blade or a cross-cut carpenter saw will cut through bear bones just fine. A steel or sharpening stone will probably be needed to hone your knife blade now and then.

Bear skinning always goes easier when two tackle the job, one to hold bear parts at advantageous angles and to pull on the hide (gloves will probably be needed to grip a slippery hide), the other to whisk the knife blade through the tissues that connect the hide to the bear.

Bear Rug Skinning

When skinning a bear, intending to have its hide made into a rug, you must end up with a complete hide having as few cuts a possible, paws and head fully attached.

Step 1— Extend the Abdominal Incision

Start by extending the abdominal incision up the center of the breastbone to the base of the neck. This will give you more freedom as you skin from the hind legs toward the head.

Step 2 — Skinning Hind Quarters

Skinning the legs properly for a bear rug is tricky. If you were to cut through the hide on the inner side of a hind leg along a straight line from the center of the bear's crotch to to the center of where its paw begins, you're going to end up with a rug that has a paw positioned at a weird angle — your cut ending up at the side of the bear's foot pad (front legs present the same problem). In order to make sure paws end up extended straight outward, your inside leg cuts must end an inch or two short of the center of the heel portion of the bear's hind foot pad. Having skinned many a bear, I know you're going to scratch your head at this point, mumbling, "How am I going to do that?"

The best way to make sure you don't ruin the appearance of your bearskin rug is to extend your inside centerline leg cuts (starting from the abdominal incision) only half way toward the paw of each leg, then skinning the lower half of each leg as if pulling off the sleeve of a tight-fitting wool sweater. Upon discovering the hide is fully intact on each lower leg, your taxidermist will be overwhelmed with joy.

The first hind leg is always the toughest to skin (everything goes much easier after that). Insert the tip of your knife — blade side up — under the hide halfway between the front and back of the bear's hind leg (ham or thigh) at the abdominal incision. Then cut through the hide on a straight line along the center of the inner leg half way to the paw. Start peeling the hide at one of the right angle corners you've created in the crotch area, lightly sweeping your knife blade across the tissues directly beneath the hide as you pull the hide back. Don't attempt to end up with a hide completely free of fat and tissue or you're liable to end up with a hide full of holes. Let your taxidermist do the fleshing. He'd much rather do this than have to patch a lot of holes. Stretching and pulling, skin the hide as far as you can around the front and back halves of the inner leg, and as far as you can around the end of your cut (around the bear's knee). Now, by forcefully bending the knee as far as it will go, you will be able to start skinning down the bear's lower leg. If the knee doesn't bend enough, carefully cut through exposed cartilages of the knee. You may have to extend your inside cut in the hide a few inches in order to cut into the knee enough to get it to bend. Skin the hide from the lower leg, rolling it down and over the paw as you go, until within a couple inches of the paw. About an inch above the edge of the rolled hide, cut into the muscles and tendons of the leg, exposing the underlying bone. With your partner holding the hide back to prevent damage from your saw blade, saw through the leg bone. Once cut, it'll be very easy to finish skinning the leg — ending up with a bear hide sack with the paw attached (intact) at the narrow end.

Be very careful when skinning around the bear's anus. That little tail directly above it is easy to cut off. Inside the tail are a series of small bones (several connected together like in a chicken neck). Carefully cut through the bone closest to the underlying rump muscle, leaving the bone intact inside the tail. When this is done, you'll be able to skin around the bear's rump with little difficulty.

Once you have one hind leg skinned, you will be able to skin completely around the bear's rump and lower back, making the other hind leg much easier to skin. Make your center cut through the hide on the inner side of other hind leg without cutting the hide of the lower leg, as before. Finally, saw off the other hind paw at the ankle, as before. Now skin the hide to the bear's forelegs.

Step 3 — Skinning Front Quarters

With your partner holding a front leg straight and fully extended, bent somewhat outward and at a right angle to the bear's body — claws parallel with the bear's breastbone and foot pad facing the same direction as the breastbone — make a right-angle cut through the hide from the incision on the bear's breastbone to the center of the inner side of a front leg and thence half way to the end of the leg. Skin this leg like a hind leg, finally cutting through the muscles, tendons and bones about three inches above the foot, keeping the paw attached. Repeat this process on the other front leg. Now continue skinning the hide from the bear's body down to the end of the cut at the base of the bear's neck.

Step 4 — Neck and Head

The hide of a black bear's short and thick neck is firmly attached. Like pulling a tight, turtle-necked sweater from the head of a human, your partner should pull the hide steadily and firmly as you carefully cut through the tough connective tissues of the neck. Skin the neck as you skinned the lower legs, making no cuts in the hide. When you can feel the angles of the bear's lower jaw beneath the fold of hide as you proceed toward the head, you've gone far enough. About an inch or two back from the fold of the hide, cut into and completely around the neck muscles and other tissues to the bear's neck bone (spine). Cut through this bone with your saw.

That's it. You're done. You now have a big, beautiful bearskin, head and paws attached, to bring to your taxidermist. If you cannot deliver the hide to your taxidermist immediately, roll it up, drop it into a large plastic bag, seal it, and store it in a freezer until delivery can be made. Do not store a bear hide in a freezer more than a few weeks or it may suffer ruinous freezer burn.

Shoulder Mount Skinning

If you are going to have a shoulder (wall) mount made, don't cut the hide anywhere forward of the back end of the rib cage. Don't extend the abdominal incision up over the breastbone as you would for a bear rug. Don't make a cut up the back of the neck as you would on a white-tailed buck. To make sure you end up with a beautiful wall mount, either skin the entire bear as you would to have a rug made (without cutting the hide over the the breastbone) — having the entire hide tanned — or provide the taxidermist with an uncut hide from the entire front half of the bear, cutting through the hide completely around the bear's body where the ribs meet the abdominal cavity. For a good shoulder mount, at least the upper half of the hide of the front legs should be attached (uncut). Also the head, of course, cut from the neck as when skinning a bear to have a rug made.

Full Body Mount Skinning

If you are thinking of a full body mount, the fewer cuts you make in the hide, the better. Though it will be tedious, skin the entire bear without making any additional cuts in the hide except those recommended for skinning hind legs (half way to paws). Do not extend the abdominal incision up over the breast bone. When you get to the front half of the bear, remove the balance of the hide as if removing a long-sleeved, tight-fitting sweater. Be especially cautious when skinning around the folds in the hide around the upper ends (elbows and armpits?) of a bear's front legs. Cut the the paws and head from the carcass as explained above.

Mounts with Snarling Lips

Should your black bear mount have snarling lips? It's a matter of personal preference, I guess. Most hunters, it seems, prefer snarling lips, enormous bear fangs bared. To those who have never hunted black bears, the visage of a snarling black bear doubtless implies the beast was truly dangerous, and the hunter who shot it was truly brave. Perhaps that's what many hunters want others to believe. Whatever, via snarling lips we hunters perpetuate the myth of the "big bad black bear."

Don't get me wrong. I have snarling bear mounts all about me as I write this — a grizzly and three blacks, one a ferocious wall mount that scares my young grandchildren. Ah well, I have little else that attests to my bravery. While some may pooh-pooh my bears with snarling lips, whether these bears ever actually snarled at me or not, it really did take every measure of bravery on my part to face them, especially when armed with a bow. Given the right to hunt them, I did nothing to endanger black bears. Acting in behalf of game managers, I helped to make sure bears in the area were not over-abundant. I helped to make sure they would not face starvation and/or diseases incumbent with overcrowding. Moreover, I played an important role in behalf of Mother Nature, cropping less-fit bears from the population, always an important step toward keeping a wild species strong. I ate those bears, making full use of a fully-renewable and delicious wild food. Moreover, I have never gazed at my snarling mounts as a conqueror. They're here because I like to look at bears; to be among them. Often, I remember them when we met, and I feel the excitement that went with those meetings. Without those snarls, they'd somehow be less that what they *really* were. These wonderful bears could never fit the mold of being benign and harmless. Nope, they simply wouldn't look right without snarls.

Butchering

For the same reasons you are unlikely to find it convenient to skin a bear, it is unlikely you will ever find it convenient to butcher a bear. However, butchers will also ask you how you want your bear cut up, so you should know something about it (for detailed home butchering instructions, see Dr. Ken Nordberg's *Whitetail Hunter's Almanac, 1st Edition*).

From a medium-to-large black bear, a butcher can make all of the cuts traditional for beef, pork or venison. All steaks or chops and roasts can be cut to look exactly like what you see in grocery stores.

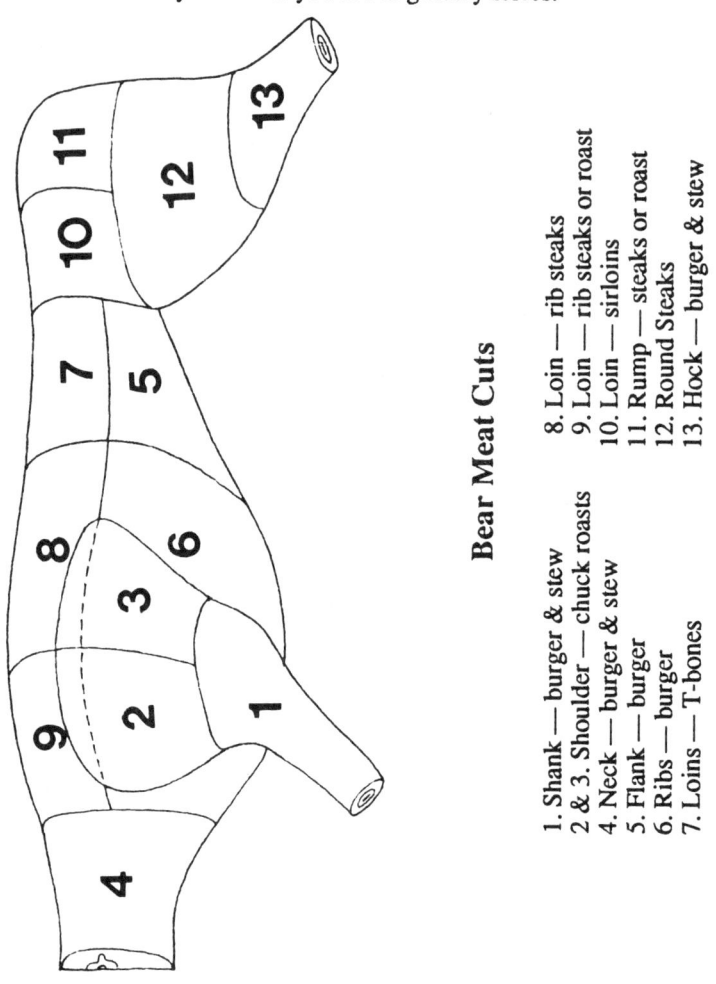

Bear Meat Cuts

1. Shank — burger & stew
2 & 3. Shoulder — chuck roasts
4. Neck — burger & stew
5. Flank — burger
6. Ribs — burger
7. Loins — T-bones
8. Loin — rib steaks
9. Loin — rib steaks or roast
10. Loin — sirloins
11. Rump — steaks or roast
12. Round Steaks
13. Hock — burger & stew

Having eaten many black bears during the past four decades, and having butchered quite a few, I have found I much prefer having my bear meat cut in a less traditional way. Here's what I'd recommend:

Loins

Loins are the long bundles of meat (back straps) extending from the base of the neck to the rump on either side of the spine. From the rib section come rib steaks or chops (whichever you prefer to call them) or rib roasts, from the abdominal section come T-bones, and from the hind quarter section come sirloins and rump roasts — all the choicest, most tender, juiciest cuts (*gold* in the freezer). I much prefer having the loins trimmed from the bone, fat removed, and cut into 1-inch steaks from end to end. If you prefer, leave the rump sections intact. They make superb roasts.

Round Steaks

Though tougher cuts, black bear round steaks are nonetheless delicious. I instruct the butcher to cut the rounds (hams) into 1-inch steaks.

Shoulders

Have shoulders cut into tradition chuck roasts, 1-1/2 - 2-inches thick with the bone left in.

Everything Else

Neck, flanks, ribs, brisket, hocks and shanks should be trimmed of fat, sinew and bone, the thicker and more tender portions cut into stew meat (you won't be able to eat enough bear stew) and the thinner or tougher portions ground. Rather than have the butcher add bear fat, pork fat or pork shoulder (meat and fat) to my ground bear meat, I much prefer the addition of one part beef fat to five parts lean bear meat. Though I like pork, to me, adding hog meat or hog fat to black bear meat is a terrible step backwards.

Black bear meat also makes wonderful sausage. Some hunters I know have their entire bears converted to various kinds of sausage.

Have the butcher wrap and quick-freeze bear meat in whatever sized portions you prefer. Tightly wrapped in freezer paper, your bear meat should remain tasty 6-12 months in the freezer. Be sure to label your bear meat so no one mistakes it for any of those lesser meats bought from a grocery store.

Trophy Bear Measurements

There was a time when hide measurements (length from nose to tail + width from front claw to front claw ÷ 2) were widely accepted as a means of determining the relative size of a bear. When it was discovered that some hunters were stretching the truth a bit — tying green hides horizontally off the ground between trees and then throwing boulders on top to stretch them — the bear skull measurement system was born. Some large bears have small heads and some small bears have large heads, so it's not the best system, but nobody thus far has figured out how to stretch a bear skull.

To qualify for the Boone and Crockett Record Book, a black bear taken by fair chase methods must have a combined length-plus-width (straight-line) skull measurement of at least 21 inches. To qualify for the Pope and Young Record Book — bow kills only — the combined score must be at least 18 inches. Skulls must be measured by official scorers to qualify, following a 60-day drying period. A black bear taken with a bow can qualify for both record books if it has a combined score of 21 inches or more.

Official scorers are common in every U.S. state. Many can be reached by inquiring at state big game management headquarters, or at state agencies that keep big game records. Information may also be obtained by writing to (or calling):

Boone and Crockett Club
241 So. Fraley Blvd.
Dumfries, VA 22026

or

Pope and Young Club
6471 Richard Ave.
Placerville, CA 95667

Bear Meat Magic

I love black bear meat. I also love venison, but I swear meat from a deepwoods (non-dump) black bear (what I call *a berry bear)* is at least ten-times better — more tasty, more tender and more juicy.

I also love bear meat for what it does to the eyebrows of people who otherwise act like you're trying to poison them when you serve wild game. With the first reluctant taste, their eyebrows raise as high as eyebrows can go. The most dedicated wild meat haters are instantly flabbergasted.

"Why, t-that's as good as beef!" they typically blurt, staring dumfounded.

"Better'n beef," I always add, grinning like a Cheshire cat.

"Yaaah," they grudgingly admit, "maybe your right. I just can't believe it. It doesn't taste even a bit gamy."

One of the delightful things about cooking softly-textured bear meat is, it doesn't dry out as easily as venison and many other wild meats. That's doubtless due to the fact that bears carry a lot of fat, meaning, their meat is somewhat marbled with fat, though certainly not to the degree expensive cuts of beef are marbled with fat. That, of course, also means bear meat is healthier than beef, containing less cholesterol.

Another delightful thing about bear meat is the flavor of its fat. It's sweet and light, unlike strong-flavored venison fat, and the fat of many other wild game animals, which contributes to gaminess. Bear fat heightens the flavor of the meat, like the fat of beef, pork, chicken or turkey. No wonder early Americans considered lard rendered from black bear fat to be the very finest for making pastries.

Unfortunately, black bear meat has a negative aspect. Like hogs, black bears are frequent hosts of the organism that causes the disease, trichinosis. Like pork, then, black bear meat must not be served pink. It must be cooked until medium to well-done.

Eyebrow-Raising Bear Steaks

Whereas I'll gladly settle for bear steaks fried in a sizzling, cast-iron skillet, nothing beats bear steaks broiled over a hot bed of charcoal. Lay them on the grill close to the heat, brown 'em on one side and then turn them over. When red juices begin oozing from the top, the steaks are medium-rare. It doesn't take long after that before they will become medium. After a minute or so, I'll cut into one with a sharp knife to check. Don't allow bear steaks to over-cook. Well-done is too-done. When just *medium*, they'll still be tender and juicy. At the magic moment, I'll sprinkle on a little salt and coarsely ground pepper and serve them promptly from the grill. If from a small-to-medium-sized bear, chances are you'll be able to cut them easily with a butter knife.

Mother Nature's Finest Stew

It is almost impossible to make a bear stew that is not good. In fact, any recipe you prefer for making beef stew is guaranteed to make a wonderful bear stew. You'll probably wonder why your beef stew never tasted as good. The following recipe, personally developed over a period of at least 30 years, will lead to unabashed groans of delight whenever bear is the basic ingredient. Being an oft requested Sunday meal whenever my kids and their families know I have bear meat in the freezer, I am usually obliged to make a large batch at a time. The following recipe will feed 14 hungry grown-ups:

- 4 lbs. black bear stew meat (cut into 1-1/2 in. cubes)
- 1/4 cup shortening
- 10 small onions (about 1-1/2 in.in diameter), peeled
- 14 medium-sized potatoes, peeled and cut into about 1-in. cubes
- 28 small-to-medium diameter carrots, peeled and cut into about 1-in. lengths
- 4 stalks celery (including leaves), cut into about 1-in. lengths
- 1/4 cup catsup
- 1/4 cup Western Dressing
- 4 Tbsp. soy sauce
- 1 Tbsp. basil
- 8 whole allspice
- 1 tsp. coarse ground pepper
- Salt to taste (2 heaping tsp. +)
- 1 cup flour
- Water as needed (about 1-1/2 qts.)

Set oven at 300°

Start by melting the shortening in a large, cast-iron or heavy aluminum roaster placed on a stove top burner set on high. Add the bear stew meat as soon as the shortening is melted, and stir briefly with a large wooden spoon. Immediately add two onions, finely sliced. With the roaster uncovered, cook the meat on high, stirring occasionally until it is all darkly browned. Turn the heat down to medium and continue cooking, stirring occasionally, until the liquid at the bottom of the roaster begins to turn medium-to-dark brown. Using tongs, remove the meat from the roaster, placing it in a bowl to one side.

Turn the burner back on high to bring the liquid in the bottom of the roaster to a vigorous boil. Scraping the bottom of the roaster frequently, boil this liquid (turn the heat down a bit if needed) until the liquid is reduced to about 1/4 inch, thick and very dark (not black — don't burn it). If it seems reluctant to darken sufficiently, add 1 tsp.. catsup, 1 tsp. Western Dressing and 1 tsp. flour, stirring vigorously until dark. Move the roaster from the burner and allow it to cool a few minutes. Now add 1-1/2 cups of water and place the roaster back on the burner (on high again). Thoroughly scrape the bottom of the roaster as the water comes to a boil.. As soon as all of the scrapings have become uniformly incorporated into the boiling water, add all of the prepared vegetables — onions, potatoes, carrots and celery. With the burner on high, liquid boiling vigorously, occasionally stir the vegetables until all are uniformly and deeply browned on the outside (this will take 20-30 minutes).

Return the meat back to the roaster and stir into the vegetables. Add enough water to raise the level of the liquid up to about one inch short the top of the meat and vegetables (burner on high).

Add one cup of flour to a pint jar, fill the jar almost to the top with cold water. Stir briefly with a fork, adding more water if necessary. Cap tightly and shake the jar vigorously 15 seconds. Set the jar aside (allowing unmixed lumps of flour to become thoroughly saturated with water).

As soon as the water in the roaster begins to boil, shake the flour/water mixture again and add it all slowly to the stew while gently stirring. Continue stirring until the liquid comes to a boil and becomes a thick gravy. If not thick enough, mix in more flour and water until the desired consistency is achieved. Now turn off the burner.

Add all remaining ingredients, stirring them gently into the stew. Don't worry about whether you have enough salt in the stew at this point. You can add more later.

Place the roaster in your 300° oven, uncovered. Cook 6-8 hours, adding water when necessary, stirring it in very gently. The uppermost meat and vegetables should protrude about 1/2 inch from the gravy at serving time. If you cook your stew in the oven overnight, turn the oven down to 250° and partially cover the roaster with foil. Turn the oven back up to 300° in the morning, adding 2-3 hours cooking time. After that, cover the roaster and keep it in the oven on "warm" until company arrives (no more stirring).

Fresh-baked honey-wheat bread (made from store-bought, frozen loaves) goes wonderfully with this stew; also fresh apple pie. The aromas from your kitchen will lure people directly to the table as they come in the front door.

Black Bear Roast

A bear roast cooked slow (325°) in a heavy covered roaster in the oven until beginning to fall apart (about 6 hours) is a delicious addition to any meal. I like to start by browning a thawed roast quickly on both sides over a stove top burner. Then all I add is a little salt, pepper and sliced onion.

Sometimes I like to add a barbecue sauce about three hours before serving. *Crazy Cajun, Hot,* is my favorite for wild game.

If you want to make a one-dish meal of it, about 1-1/2 hours before serving, place the roaster on a stove top burner on high, removing the meat. Add a little water to the drippings and brown peeled potatoes, carrots and onions cut in halves or quarters lengthwise in the roaster. As soon as the vegetables are browned, add salt, pepper, 4 whole allspice and a half bay leaf, stirring slightly. Then put the roast on top of the vegetables and place the roaster back in the oven uncovered, turning the oven up to 350° for about one hour or until the vegetables are tender when probed with a fork.

Ground Bear

Whatever recipe you use that requires ground beef, ground bear will make it better, bear spaghetti and bear chili being among the best. My "Sveetie" prefers bearburgers over all others. Here's how I make them:

Form ground bear into 1/2-pound patties about 3/4-inch thick. Fry or broil (in the oven or over charcoal) until medium-done. After turning (one side browned), spoon over the top a half-and-half mixture of Bullseye Barbecue Sauce and Western Dressing (adding Western Dressing to meat might sound crazy, but when cooked it becomes a wonderful wild game sauce). Then add a large, thin slice of onion (Jene likes her onion partially cooked). When the meat is done, place it between slices of toasted bread or in a toasted sesame seed bun; then enjoy.

After trying these recipes, I know your bear meat isn't going to last long. You'll probably even start telling friends and relatives begging for bear meat that you're out when your freezer is still half full. When you *do* run out, you'll begin to crave bear meat, telling others more and more about how delicious it is. Before you know it you'll be asking someone, "Hey, when's the deadline for getting bear hunting permit applications in?"

Epilogue

It Doesn't Get Any Better

Nine feet above the ground, a basketball-sized swarm of wasps, heavy with honey purloined from logs below, buzzed languidly from side-to-side, reluctant to give up the warmth of the bright beam of golden sunset angling horizontally through the darkening evergreens. Three feet from the wasps, a camouflaged hunter sat frozen, his head pressed tightly back against the trunk of an ancient balsam tree. Noting the wasps were slowly drawing nearer, the hunter gazed at the beam of light, gauging its relentless, swinging progress.

"What next?" he muttered to himself. *"Something always seems to go wrong when hunting big bears. This is a new one. I've never been run out of a stand by wasps before."*

Big bears were his quarry, all right, more precisely, *one big bear*. It was a black bear he figured would go well over 400 pounds, judging by the length of its hind prints, and long-range glimpses he'd had during previous months — during previous years, actually. The season before, at least three hunters had started out determined to take this bear, but the bear — a big boar — had outfoxed them all, never approaching a bait pit by day and then keeping hunters guessing by staying away for days at a time. Now, the bear was up to his old tricks. The hunter's son had waited patiently in this stand during the previous two days without seeing a bear.

"This will be the evening he comes," the hunter had concluded over breakfast that morning. *"It all adds up. This is his pit. Dousing the clearing with urine, he's kept all other bears away. That's a sign of a dominant boar, likely the largest bear in this area. Though it had been visiting the pit regularly during the previous two weeks of baiting, something or someone had driven it away. If it took to its accustomed foraging route, a route that would take it five miles east and five miles west, it will take three days before that bear will pass this way again. Today's the day!"*

The hunter stalked silently to his stand six hours before sunset, his rubber boots generously painted with fox urine. His trail would not carry the message of freshness, fox urine further confounding the bear's sensitive nose. For five hours the hunter endured, stoically biding his time without motion or sound. Now it was the witching hour — the last hour before sunset. The west wind had died, an occasional, barely-audible sigh in the balsams now. Bears like it calm, their ears able to detect the merest whisper. Silence is golden to a bear — safety; security. A bear could afford to be less cautious now. A normally nocturnal bear might even decide it's safe to visit a bait pit before sunset. If it did, it would have to be soon.

"Within 30 minutes," the hunter noted, glancing nervously toward his watch.

Witching hour or not, the swarm of wasps was drawing ever nearer. Hind legs dangling, they danced only eighteen inches before the hunter's unblinking face. The hunter didn't realize the wasps were unwitting allies, pinning him like a statue against the tree. The hunter had not noticed the creature that had silently emerged from the deep grass of a black ash slough 75 yards east, the creature that was now directing its extraordinary senses toward the very balsam in which the hunter sat.

All at once the shaft of sunlight streaming over the hunter's left shoulder faded and the wasps were gone, but hunter's eyes didn't move. Within his same exact line of vision stood a bear...a *monster* bear. Realization struck like a prairie rattler. The hunter's heart lurched, thumping more loudly than he had ever known before.

For several moments, the hunter's experience failed him. Paralyzed, he stared in awe. This was clearly the largest bear he had ever seen in the wilds. It's smallish ears were set wide, its neck was massive and it's rump was steer-wide. Its belly hung low to the ground and its legs were like nail kegs. This was truly a big bear, a beautiful bear, its fur jet-black and thick. Obviously a mighty bear too, bristling with dominance and enormous strength — a king of bears. The hunter could only guess its weight.

"Four-hundred pounds?" he wondered. *"Five-hundred?"*

The bear began to move, striding silently with a peculiar, high-stepping grace toward the hunter. The hunter's body tensed. His hands unconsciously squeezed the bow resting across his lap. The shaft of his nocked arrow slipped from its moleskin-lined arrow rest.

Snap!

The bear abruptly halted, mid-stride, lifting its massive head toward the origin of the sound. Wincing inside, the hunter held his breath — unblinking eyes directed downward — hoping (no, praying) his errant sound would not spell doom.

Hands quivering now, the hunter began to will himself to concentrate on what he must do. The bear became a mere dark shadow at the edge of his field of vision as his eyes focused on the bow in his lap.

"As soon as I can," he began planning, *"I'll have to ease my back away from the tree. That bear will surely hear clothing rubbing against the bark. I'll have to keep my eyes on my hands, first while I ease my arrow back onto my rest, then as I hook up my release and finally as I go through the entire process of raising my bow for the shot. It's a good thing I rehearsed doing it. Now I know I'll have to swing my lower bow limb wide to safely clear that metal platform brace next to my left leg."*

The bear turned to its right and began circling the bait pit fifty-yards out, slipping silently and effortlessly through interlaced alders and upraised branches of windfalls. The hunter waited sixty seconds after the bear passed from his field of vision before slowly turning his head. The bear was gone.

"Where'd he go?" the hunter pondered. *"I hope he's only checking my trail, still intending to come in. Doing that would be only natural for this bear. I'd better get ready. It might return at any moment."*

Upon easing his back from his stand tree, the hunter carefully moved the shaft of his arrow to its proper position and attached his release to his bow string beneath the arrow's nock. He then slowly raised the upper limb of his bow to a 45° angle — as much as he could do until ready to begin his draw and take aim.

Several minutes passed before the hunter thought he heard a sound — the rustle of grass. Back arched, ears intent, body frozen, the hunter riveted his eyes on a spot to the right of the bait pit. Moments later, a dark shadow moved into his field of vision from directly beneath his stand platform, heading directly toward the log-covered bait pit.

"He did just what I figured. He came right up my trail. Oh-oh, he's facing me. I won't be able to move."

The bear dipped its massive head and began noisily lapping honey from the logs covering the bait pit.

"Sounds just like a dog lapping water. Oops...he's looking up at me."

Mouth closed to keep his heart beats from being heard by the bear only five yards away, the hunter concentrated on avoiding discernable chest movements.

"He's lapping again, but still facing in my direction. I'm doing all right so far. My camo must be all right. I sure wish he'd turn though. I don't know how long I can stand this. Oh-oh, now he's looking up at me again."

Upon lapping the last of the honey, the bear stepped to the top of the logs.

"My gosh...he's longer than the logs!"

After a brief glance about the clearing, the bear inserted a paw into a crack and with a thunderous clatter swept two 100-pound-plus logs from the pit. Reaching down with its tawny muzzle, it picked out an ear of sweet corn and stepped to the left of the pit, facing away from the hunter, quartering to the left. Pinning the ear of corn to the ground with its right paw, it began to strip away the green husk with its incisors. Realizing he was at last safe from the eyes of the bear, the hunter turned his head a bit.

"Perfect! You can't get a better shot angle than that."

Eyes now intent on his bow, the hunter began to slowly raise his left arm, the upper limb of the bow rising to a vertical position. Then the hunter began his draw, his eyes watching the shaft of his metal arrow as it silently eased back over its padded rest. Shortly, the the hunter's right thumb nestled against the angle of his jaw. Turning a bit from the waist, the bear — now contentedly nibbling kernels of corn from the cob — became fully visible within the fuzzy-edged circle of the hunter's string peep sight. It was still facing away, quartering to the left.

"Okay...bead in center of peep...bead half way down, one inch to the right of the bear's last rib...take in a slow breath...hold it...index finger over release trigger...squeeze."

WHAP!

The hunter saw his bright blue and green fletchings disappear into the exact spot at which he had aimed. Instantly, the bear tore from the bait pit clearing through parting, four-foot ferns and hazels. Quickly glancing at his watch, the hunter peered anxiously north, taking note of landmarks along the path of the recklessly plunging bear, now battering its way through loudly-snapping swamp alders. Suddenly it was totally silent. Fifteen seconds had passed. Then twenty.

ar-r-AUGH...ar-r-AUGH...ar-r...

"You did it!" the hunter cried, now grinning from ear-to-ear. *"Oh man, was that something!"* Knees shaking uncontrollably now, the hunter leaned back and took in a deep breath, gazing upward at the evening sky. *"Wow, a monster bear with a bow,"* the hunter laughed, shaking his head. *"From only five yards, yet. I did everything right. For that bear, everything had to be right. This was the best. The absolute best. It just doesn't get any better."*

That's black bear hunting — the story of how I took a Pope and Young black bear last Labor Day (see color photo section).

Study this book well, my friend. The future of the black bear and black bear hunting lies firmly in your hands. May you be a worthy match for this wonderful, precious animal.

Good hunting,

Doc

Bibliography

Nolan, Wade and Ralph Ertz, *Bowhunting Hungry Black Bears*, Girdwood, Alaska Wilderness Perspective, 1988. A hunting video with black bear natural history by Gary Alt, Pennsylvania black bear researcher.

Rogers, Lynn L., *Wildlife Monographs 97*, Blacksburg, 1987. Effects of food supply and kinship on social behavior, movements, and population growth of black bears in northeastern Minnesota: 1–72.

Smith, Richard P., *The Book of the Black Bear*, Piscataway, Winchester Press, 1985.

Wise, Sherry, *The Black Bear (PUBL-WM015 85)*, Madison, Wisconsin Department of Natural Resources, 1986.

Other valuable paperback hunting guides by Dr. Ken Nordberg:

WHITETAIL HUNTER'S ALMANAC
2nd Edition

An intriguing, step-by-step guide to hunting adult whitetailed bucks, September through December. Based on 21 years of unique, "wild" whitetail behavioral studies. A "bestseller" nationwide. **$7.95**

WHITETAIL HUNTER'S ALMANAC
1st Edition

A comprehensive guide to deer signs, key buck and doe home range elements, productive stand sites, effective calling and rattling, using lure scents, low-profile hunting, big-buck-effective stand hunting, still-hunting, drives, home butchering and much more. **$7.95**

To be published soon (August, 1990):
$7.95
WHITETAIL HUNTER'S ALMANAC
3rd Edition, featuring
"The Deadliest Technique: *Mobile* Stand Hunting"
$7.95

To order, send check or money order (U.S. funds) to: Dr. Ken Nordberg, 6912 Logan Avenue N., Brooklyn Center, MN 55430. **Include $1.00 for postage and mailer ($1.50 Canada).** MN residents add $.48 tax.